Refocusing the Evangelical Mind

A Call to Return to Biblical Beliefs and Behavior

Roger C. Palms

Refocusing the Evangelical Mind
A Call to Return to Biblical Beliefs and Behavior

Copyright © 2014 Roger C. Palms
All rights reserved.
Unless otherwise indicated, all Scripture is taken from the New International Version of the Bible: Scripture taken from the HOLY BIBLE, NEW INTERNATIONAL VERSION ®. NIV®. COPYRIGHT © 1973, 1978, 1984, 2011 by Biblica, Inc.®. Used by permission. All rights reserved worldwide.

ISBN: 1494724170
ISBN 13: 9781494724177
Library of Congress Control Number: 2013923202
CreateSpace Independent Publishing Platform
North Charleston, South Carolina

Confession to my Fellow Believers...

I love the family of God, the faithful brothers and sisters in Christ for whom I pray and who pray for me. There is a oneness in Christ that is stronger and more beautiful than any other relationship—even the warmth of the natural family. The company of the redeemed, the people of the Way, are a people who can understand and relate to the deepest longings and joys of the heart.

So writing about any weaknesses in the body of believers is painful. Many times I thought I should not point out where we seem to be cluttering up the Gospel with matters that draw attention away from Christ. But too many evangelical Christians, those who know the One who is the way, the truth and the life, are adding their own content to the Gospel and those additions are alienating men and women who need to hear the truth about Jesus and understand His redemptive work.

From fellow believers I keep hearing angry rants against the culture, their fears that Christianity is in a losing battle with secularism. We who are believers live in two cultures, the one around us and the one to which we and the redeemed of the world belong. But too many of us are covering over the eternal truths with secular lies that we are convinced are about matters that are real. It is our lies that turn people away from the Savior.

I confess my love for those who acknowledge believing, biblical faith in Christ. But I also confess the pain, the hurt that comes, when I seek to meet my secular friends where they are with the Good News that I know they need to hear. I listen to these lost ones who are not complete without Christ demonstrating their emptiness; it is an emptiness that I know our God in Christ can fill.

These secular men and women think they already know about me, an evangelical Christian. Yet what they know about me has nothing to do with Jesus. It has everything to do with the false teachings Christians proclaim that cover over that much-needed Good News. Some Christians may think they are being rejected for their belief in Jesus. But much of the time that rejection isn't about Jesus at all. It is about what we have added to Jesus that is untrue but that so many believers do not realize is untrue.

What follows in these pages is about me as much as it is about anyone else.

Introduction

I made a big switch in my thinking.

At first, this book was intended to show the limits, the mental poverty of so many secular people who live in their own bubble comfortably unchallenged by Christians who either back away or go to war with them. I wanted to point out the ways that the Gospel can and should reach people who are without hope and missing the peace of God that is in Christ.

The secular mind hasn't changed. The need of those who think they are broad minded, not religious—but who in fact show that they are very religious and closed minded as they try to fashion their own "faith" that suits themselves—is just as strong as it has always been. But to many, the people of evangelical faith who have what the secular person is missing are no longer offering the biblical truth that unbelievers need. We have traded "saviors," and the secular person doesn't want those other saviors we are offering.

My thinking changed when I kept running into the Christian mind that creates so much in the way of un-Christian or non-Christian thought. We have become known as people who no longer think and are unable to articulate biblical Christianity. Indeed, we have covered over God's redeeming message so that the light of the Good News can no longer be seen through the trappings we have added; we are preventing the secular man and woman from seeing God's truth in Christ.

So we who claim the name of Jesus, who assume that we are rejected, even despised, for our Christian faith, are too often being rejected and despised for the false religion we have adopted and proclaim that has nothing to do with Jesus.

The secular mind still has its limits, and we will see those limits in these pages. But the secular person is not an unreachable person. We will see how clearly-presented biblical faith can respond to and reach out to those who are still bound by their secular limits.

Yet we will not hide what we as evangelicals have done to prevent others from seeing the Savior. It is a painful story, but it must be told.

That is the reason for this book.

Refocusing the Evangelical Mind

Table of Contents

Confession to my Fellow Believers…	iii
Introduction	v
chapter 1: Our Cluttered Gospel	1
chapter 2: What They See Is What They Get	23
chapter 3: Lying: A Christian Virtue?	43
chapter 4: Following the Media Propagandists	63
chapter 5: Forgetting Our History (Christian and American)	95
chapter 6: Presenting Good News to Secular Minds	131
chapter 7: While There Is Still Time	153
chapter 8: Letting the Light Shine	187
chapter 9: All Truth Is God's Truth— but We May Be Missing It	203
chapter 10: Ready for Tomorrow	233

chapter 1

Our Cluttered Gospel

One day in Israel, after my wife, Andrea, and I had planted a tree in celebration of our 25th anniversary, the arborist who was there told us about a museum just across the road, the Golani Brigade Commemoration Site. So we went across the road to see it and were met by a guide who would explain to us all that was being memorialized there. We had just started walking when he turned to me and asked, "Are you a Christian?" I replied, "Yes, I am." Then he stopped, looked me in the eye and asked, "But are you a believing Christian?"

Now I know there is no such thing as an unbelieving Christian. But I knew what he meant. Am I a Christian in name only? Am I a follower of the Christ? He knew there was a difference between those who only claim the name and those who also live the life.

For many, the picture of Jesus that we present to others is out of focus. It is blurred. As a result, not only is it difficult for the person looking at the picture to understand what he is seeing, but the blurry picture is irritating to him. If we want others to know the Savior, it is time to refocus the picture that we are presenting.

Slander from Another Pew

It was Sunday morning and we were seated as the worship service in our church was about to begin. I was praying quietly, preparing my heart for worship. Then, behind me, I heard a man talking rather loudly to the person seated next to him. He was explaining that recently he had heard a sermon about how the Hebrew king Abimelech led his country to destruction and how President Obama was leading America down the same road, step by step. Then he explained that it is really the president's wife who runs the country because the president doesn't know how. This man went on to tell his listener that Michelle Obama earns $40,000 per month and will run for president next time. Then he mentioned a few other points about the decline in America. The man he was speaking to was so interested that he asked how he could get a copy of that preacher's sermon. Then, with that man's words still ringing in my mind, we were called to worship God.

That man seated behind me, with his information, wasn't the first to speak that way, whether in church or out, at worship or not. Many of my fellow believers seem eager to tell me—and anyone else who will listen—how evil other people are, particularly those in the government administration. So many Christians, particularly evangelicals, are willing to list the evils occurring around us in our culture and in Washington DC, evils that are bringing our nation to the brink of disaster. I hear Christians trotting out one popular urban legend after another, all pointing to what is sending us to destruction.

I wanted to reply to that man who was sitting behind me, as I hope to reply to others. But we weren't in a private place where I could do that. We were in church, and with all of that hatefulness ringing in my ears I was being called to worship God. I wanted to say two things to that man. I wanted to tell him that, "You certainly know a lot of things that aren't true." And I wanted to ask him to go home, make a long list of all the evils in our society that are so shocking to him. I wanted to encourage him to write down all those evils, real or perceived, that are happening now, the ones he feels are destroying our country. Then, when he had completed his list and could think of no more evil, I would ask him to take a large, red-felt pen and write across his list: "All this has happened on my watch."

On My Watch

On my watch, all the deterioration that angers and frightens so many believers has happened. On my watch, people have slipped into decadence and debauchery. On my watch, laws have changed and practices in contrast to Scripture have been endorsed.

But also on my watch, many Christians have stopped obeying the teachings of the Lord whom they learn about in church and praise in their worship. And the world has seen our hypocrisy. Those outside of Christ, with longings for something to fill their empty souls, are watching and seeing little that is attractive about us or the Savior we proclaim. We have hidden the light of the Gospel under a bushel. The people who walk in darkness are unable to see the great light. What they see is what we present to them—and too often it is quite ugly.

The apostle Peter is hard hitting. He wrote, "So put away all malice and all deceit and hypocrisy and envy and all slander. Like newborn infants, long for the pure spiritual milk that by it you may grow up to salvation—if indeed you have 'tasted that the Lord is good.' As you come to him, a living stone rejected by men but in the sight of God chosen and precious, you yourselves like living stones are being built up as a spiritual house" (1 Pet. 2:1–5, ESV).

"But," I can hear someone say, "Can't I slander the congressman I don't like? Can't I be critical of a president I didn't vote for? That's what we do when we Christians get together for a barbecue or after church." My reply is, "Sure, you can. But not if you want to grow up, not if you want to be a building stone in God's spiritual house, not if you want to stop living as a spiritual baby and grow in the Lord instead."

Unwrapping Jesus

How do we unwrap Jesus from what has been put on Him socially, culturally and politically? How can we reach people who have only heard about a Christian faith that is different from what Jesus taught? How do we reach the unsaved who think they already know what Christianity is because they have met vocal, angry Christians?

Idolatry is the act of putting something else in the place of God. We hear Christians arguing, "We aren't rejecting Jesus; we are good citizens and we have to protect our nation from evil leaders. We would have fought against a Hitler." But that's hindsight. At the time of Hitler, most Christians in Germany weren't fighting against him. They embraced him because he corrected many problems of their day politically, economically and socially. In our selective process today, we may be thinking that we are rejecting a bad political ideology while embracing a good one. But either one is still idolatry.

There is fear among secular people that political Christians will destroy America. What we see as helping our nation is seen by others as taking away our democracy. They see the refusal of many right-wing Christians to work within our culture and government for good, and who offer the belief that they will never work with or help our democracy. Instead, we are seen as not wanting a true democracy but a theocracy with only the right-wing Christians deciding how that theocracy will work. No wonder we are feared as being anti-American.

People who know about the Crusades in the Middle Ages and about the slaughter of Protestants in France under Catholic kings, as well as other unsavory events in history, can't be blamed for fearing the results of a renewed anger, a hateful spirit that is being broadcast by too many evangelicals today.

Instead of being willing to have a level playing field where all views are tolerated and people are allowed their own beliefs, many Christians have decided that our national beliefs must only be Christian because to them that is the view that is biblically correct. But those Christians who think of themselves as biblically correct are often the same ones who not only will violate the rights of others in the country but will violate biblical teachings as well in order to accomplish their goals.

What Our Country Used to Be

We are seen as a people who will settle for nothing less than getting our own way. We cry, "But our country isn't what it used to be," by selecting the positives and ignoring the negatives of our history—not by seeing what we used to be but by selecting what we think we used to be.

One day, at a civic luncheon, I was sitting next to an African-American man as we listened to a speaker who kept repeating the words, "We have to take the country back to what it used to be." After hearing that for the fifth or sixth time, I leaned over to my friend and asked, "Would you like the country to get back to what it used to be?" He gave me a tight-lipped, "What do you think?"

How do I get past what others are screaming so loudly so that I can point people to the Savior? What I have to do is somehow undo what other Christians have done when they have replaced Jesus with something else.

In an article in the July 15, 2013, edition of *alife*, the publication of the Christian and Missionary Alliance, I read the words of Shane Claiborne who told an interviewer: "I grew up in the Bible

Belt, so we heard a lot about Jesus. But then I started to look at the church and feel like there is a big difference between being a fan of Jesus and being a follower, being a believer in Jesus and a disciple. In fact, I started to see a lot of contradictions in the church I grew up in.

"When studying sociology, I saw a lot of disturbing things. Sociological studies show that the higher a person's church attendance, often the more prone they are to be racist, sexist, anti-gay, pro-war, pro-death penalty, and known for a lot of things that Jesus wasn't known for. I really began to wrestle with that stuff."

My antenna is always up; I try to look at my fellow believers from the perspective of those who don't know Jesus. If I go to a person to talk about the Savior, what is he really hearing? Does he know that I am a follower of the God of love? Does he know that I am a person who is trying to follow the Prince of Peace? Does he know that I am an ambassador with a message of redemption and heaven? Or does he assume that I am a hateful person who only wants to tell other people how they ought to live and demand that they practice my Christian principles in their lives.

Kicking God out of America

I teach Christian writers, some young but mostly middle-aged; some are from other countries, but most are living in the U.S. I encourage them to write their passion, and they do. A few of my students want to get published because they are angry and worried and want to get their message out to the country as a whole.

My job as a mentor is not to correct their views, because they have a right to their views, but to help them substantiate what they are saying and clearly write what they think. But some just want to throw out their statements wildly and emotionally. I wonder how the lost people will react to some of the writing that I'm seeing.

For example, I read, "The leftist atheists are trying to kick God out of America." So I have to say to that student, "I didn't know anybody could kick God anywhere."

Is that writer a follower of some puny god of our own making who can be pushed around by us or other people? Or is this the Omnipotent, Omnipresent, Omniscient and Eternal God of the universe about whom we are talking? Do any of us have the power to "Kick God out of America" or "Put God back in America"? Is our God that small?

One student, a new grandmother who is very concerned for her grandchildren growing up in America, is alarmed at what she sees happening in this country. In her writing she referred several times to our right to freedom of religion. "We have a right to freedom of religion and that is being taken away from us." Then she writes, "Christians have to make this a Christian country." I tried to show her that she really had two different articles. One is about the freedom of religion we are guaranteed and one is about making this a Christian country. Does freedom of religion mean that Christians have a right to be the only rulers in America? Freedom of religion is about equal laws protecting all religions.

This woman also wrote that "America is 78 percent Christian; we have to take America back from the masses." I needed to point out to her that if, indeed, we are 78 percent Christian, as she said, then we already are the masses.

She concluded one of her articles with a prayer. It is worth reading aloud. Try to picture an unsaved person, a secular person, who is a patriot and who loves his country, hearing or reading this prayer. She prayed, *"O Lord, this is your country. But the liberal atheists are driving you out of your country. Give us the strength and the courage to bring you back to your country."*

So I had to ask, when did America become God's country? Where in Scripture does it say that? Is God a weak god whom we can manipulate at will and either "drive Him out" or "bring Him back?" Is this the God we want to announce to our lost world?

Always I have to think, "How is this being heard by the people with whom I want to talk about the Savior? Will lost people be more likely or less likely to be interested in our Christ if this is what they hear from us?"

What Scripture will lift people to a higher plane so that they can see Jesus and understand why He came to die for us? How can we explain why He rose again for us? How do we present our Christian message so that it can be heard and distinguished from the clutter that we have added to the Gospel?

When speaking with a person who is not a follower of Jesus, I find myself trying to turn the conversation away from what he already "knows" Christianity is all about to, "Let's look at what God says." And I try to move on to the Scriptures and away from the angry-sounding Christians who make their own political and social biases the same as what the Bible teaches.

For example, I read in the Bible, "Let this mind be in you, which was also in Christ Jesus..." (Phil. 2:5, KJV). I talk with my unsaved friends about what Jesus came to do for each of us based on who He is and what He taught, which is often very different from what other evangelicals have been telling them.

We can point to God's majesty. We can point to the Gospel message that is based not on political or social stories but on our own stories and what we experienced when we came to saving faith. Unless, of course, we don't want to speak of the Redeemer, only about what we can do to preserve a nation and a culture that is troubling us.

Smash Muslims

One day I was talking with an active church woman who was angry about Muslims. When I said we needed to pray for the Muslim people, she replied, "They don't understand prayer. We have to smash them. That's the only thing they understand." And when the Boston marathon bomber was caught and was in the hospital wounded, it was a conservative, not a liberal, who was on television saying that the nineteen-year-old man under guard should be tortured.

That got me to thinking about how Muslims are perceived and how Christians are perceived in secular society. Are secular people seeing both Christians and Muslims the same way?

The average Muslim will explain, "I'm a person of prayer. I believe in strong family values. I am a person of peace."

To which the reply comes from the frightened, angry people: "No, you're not. You pray for my destruction. You put women down. Your idea of peace is a time when everyone becomes a Muslim. Otherwise you will attack and destroy us. You are out to take over my country. You want to rewrite our laws and rule us by your Sharia law. Deep down inside you are all Taliban Muslims."

The Christian also says, "I'm a person of prayer. I believe in strong family values. I am a person of peace." To which comes the reply: "No, you're not. You pray for everyone to be like you. You put people down who disagree with you; you aren't a person of peace. I've heard what you say. You are a people of hate. You want to take us over with your Christian version of laws written your way. You want to destroy America and our freedoms. You want to take away our freedom of religion and make the country accept only your religion. Deep down inside you are all Taliban Christians."

We have established for ourselves a reputation that makes it difficult to talk about Jesus, who He is and what He taught.

When Jesus was talking with a Samaritan woman next to a well, she wanted to turn the conversation to their differences: You Jews believe this; we Samaritans believe that. Jesus didn't go down that road. He began to talk to her about living water (see John 4:11–26). Living water is our message too. He alone can quench people's thirst for God. Jesus kept coming back to what was important for that Samaritan woman to know. His teaching wasn't about which political, social, or religious view was correct—His or hers. It was about Himself, the true living water. That's our message too.

My Political View Doesn't Save

When Christians wrap Jesus into their own political and social views, we then have an uphill battle with others in our society because people need to see Jesus as Savior, not as a member of a political party.

The apostle Paul didn't rant and rave and demand change within the Roman powers. He dealt with the more serious issues of people and their soul needs. What did he do day after day? "For this reason, since the day we heard about you, we have not stopped praying for you. We continually ask God to fill you with the knowledge of his will through all the wisdom and understanding that the Spirit gives" (Col. 1:9). Where in that prayer does he talk about all political wisdom and understanding?

Wait! Aren't we to be concerned for the political events that shape our nation and make an impact on the lives of citizens? Of course, but we don't make that a substitute for what is biblically important. We don't communicate to the culture that our political feelings not the greater truths of God are of primary importance. Neither do we communicate that our political views and our biblical teaching are the same and that to accept the one is the same as accepting the other. Or, worse, if they will accept what we consider to be the proper political position, they don't even need the Savior.

When we mix our social and political views with the teachings of Jesus and shout those views out in an angry tone of voice and communicate that we are speaking these things on behalf of God, the person listening becomes confused as to what Christianity is. And how will angry Christians handle Matthew 12:36? There Jesus said, "We will give account on the day of judgment for every careless word we have spoken"? Is that true? Every careless word? Are we prepared to someday explain our careless words and even our lies to the One who judges?

No Longer Christian

I remember a man who worked in the trades. He was a union man and a Democrat. He was also a serious, Bible-believing Christian. He served on the board of his evangelical church and was highly respected for his walk with Christ. But then came the time of a presidential election.

One day, at church, someone rushed up to this man and breathlessly exclaimed that some vandals had placed a sticker on his car promoting the Democratic candidate for president. This man replied, "Oh, it wasn't vandals. I put it there. I'm voting for that man."

That did it. For those evangelicals, anyone who voted for the Democratic Party candidate couldn't possibly be a Christian. In the months that followed he and his family were shunned; he was eased off the board of the church and eventually the family left that church. They then attended another evangelical church where the people didn't know that they had voted for the Democratic ticket.

From then on this man had to do what many other evangelicals have to do—he and his family had to live a double life. They said nothing about politics while all the time listening to their Christian brethren denouncing their party as anti-Christian and the other party as the Christian party. Had the church been honest, they may have found that this man who followed Jesus was way ahead of others in his Christian faith. He wasn't putting Democrats and Christians on an equal footing as though either one is the same as the other. He knew the difference between the One who saves and a political party that doesn't in a way that many of his fellow Christians did not.

We are a called-out people, a royal priesthood. Why do we toss that aside to be just like others in the secular society who are not a part of the company of the redeemed? We are urged by the apostle Paul, "Follow God's example, therefore, as dearly loved children and walk in the way of love, just as Christ loved us and gave himself up for us as a fragrant offering and sacrifice to God" (Eph. 5:1–2).

Do I Have a Christian Worldview?

Don't I have a right to present my Christian worldview?

Yes, but do I even have a Christian worldview? Or do I have my own worldview that I have baptized? Is my worldview any different than that of the unsaved people around me? David Noebel, author of *Understanding the Times,* says that a worldview is "…any ideology, philosophy, theology, movement or religion that provides an overarching approach to understanding God, the world and man's relations to God and the world."

The "Focus on the Family" website gives reference to a survey by the Barna research group. It showed, "…only 4 percent of Americans had a 'biblical' worldview." When they looked at born-again believers, the number was nine percent. A worldview provides the framework by which we make sense of our lives and the world. The Barna group showed, "…most Americans have little idea how to integrate core biblical principles to form a unified and meaningful response to the challenges and opportunities of life."

Since we are to be people who offer other people the message of the Redeemer, isn't it our role to follow Jesus in every dimension of our lives? Or can we serve God and some form of mammon? What did the apostle Paul state to believers in his day when many were suffering, even being martyred under the notorious Nero? Paul wrote, "Let everyone be subject to the governing authorities, for there is no authority except that which God has established. The authorities that exist have been established by God. Consequently, whoever rebels against the authority is rebelling against what God has instituted, and those who do so will bring judgment on themselves" (Rom. 13:1–2).

Paul knew how to integrate a biblical worldview into life as he found it. If we believe that God is the ruler of the universe, we understand that passage of Scripture. If we believe that God is ruler except in the place where we live and that we must fight for Him against sinful leaders, we have either forgotten who the mighty God is or we have limited Him to be a "sometimes God" who must have our help with His rule over the world. Our worldview, based on who we are biblically in Christ, is what should be governing our lives.

Religion Is Dangerous

A man who does not profess to follow Jesus told me, "Religion is dangerous." He based that belief on militant Islam and what he sees as militant Christianity. Who can blame him? What has he seen of Jesus in our cluttered Gospel? When we claim to be followers of Jesus and then follow everything else instead, our words about Jesus are not just empty, they may be destructive. The person who rejects Christ because he sees that following

Jesus means practicing militant behavior probably thinks that we are proof of what Christianity is all about.

Is that secular person consistent or even logical in his own beliefs? No, he too looks for examples to support what he already wants to believe. As one scientist said of those searching for hominids, the predecessors of man, "To a person looking to prove that hominids existed, every scrap of bone he finds is the bone of a hominid." The secular person finds evidence for what he has already decided to believe. But it is too often the same with Christians. We are good at finding evidence for what we are already certain is true, especially about cultural or political things.

In time our partisanship can become addictive. Liking or hating one group or another, one political party or another, if built upon over time will make a person always seek the "pleasure" that comes from additional reinforcement of that belief. Like drug addicts, we begin to need our next fix.

A Call down the Centuries

We read the words of the prophet Isaiah, "Every valley shall be raised up, every mountain and hill made low; the rough ground shall become level, the rugged places a plain." Then we read, "And the glory of the LORD will be revealed, and all people will see it together" (Isaiah 40:4–5).

But will the glory of the Lord be revealed? In a very real sense, with the incarnation, that glory has been revealed already. But will all mankind together see it if we have done the opposite to what we are called to do in Isaiah's prophetic pronouncement?

When I read about a man like Noah, I see that he walked with God. Do I walk with God? Noah was focused, he was righteous and he was "…blameless among the people of his time" (Gen. 6: 9). That's the way the people who lived around him saw him. How do the people who live around me see me?

When the people who live around me see the clutter that has been put around the Gospel, I might try to ignore or circumvent that clutter. Or I can realize that this is a very emotional issue for people and all I can say is, "I know what you are hearing and seeing among vocal Christians, but where Christians have sounded militant and hateful to you, they didn't learn that from Jesus." Then I try to turn the conversation around to who Jesus is and what He taught because usually an apology for the false ideas that person has heard isn't enough. The clutter we have added to the Gospel, our social, cultural and political additions, will still be there in the mind of the unbeliever even as we try to introduce him to biblical truth.

The Judgment of Me

If I fill my mind with what is not true, believing the hateful words of my favorite talking heads on radio and television and then quoting them to others as if what I repeat is biblically correct while ignoring the chance to tell the real truth about Jesus, how will I answer to God when I am called to give account for my behavior?

When Christians wrap Jesus up in their own political and social views, we then have an uphill battle because we want people to see Jesus as Savior but others hear only what the vocal Christians among us are saying, which rarely has anything to do with the Savior.

When I go to a person with the Good News, I find that I have to cut through the reputation that we evangelical Christians have as being nasty, people haters, even demanders of our own political rights or positions. Overcoming that is very hard to do.

I read in Scripture, "Peace I leave with you; my peace I give you. I do not give to you as the world gives" (John 14:27). We are to be people who offer other people the message of the redeeming Christ, not the message of a political party's teaching that creates a hindrance and distraction to what is biblically important. If we don't, then we are no different message bearers than those the world offers.

If I am being a person who brings peace, that means I need to take down any anger-filled barriers that I or other Christians have erected and come alongside an unsaved person with the saving message of Jesus. My approach is an arm-around-the-shoulder approach, not a throwing-words-out-over-a-wall approach.

I am told by Jesus to: "Love the Lord your God with all your heart and with all your soul and with all your mind....Love your neighbor as yourself" (Matt. 22:37–39). Would I attack myself in the same way that I attack other people who are not like me? Can I attack another person while all the time stating that I love God? Can I separate those two parts of Jesus' commandment?

The Need to Be Clear Minded

Are secular people more "clear minded" than Christians? They are not. Those who make a god of their own reason are usually very unreasonable about it. They have faith in their own ability to reason, but that is a faith in something that they have created themselves—it doesn't really exist. We have to know that what many unsaved people associate with the Christian faith may have nothing to do with the Bible or with the saving work of Jesus. Since what they believe is what they have already decided to believe, they are not yet willing to surrender the god that they have created for the God who has revealed Himself in Jesus.

That's the way most of us were as well before being captured by the Living Word of God. I did not come easily into the kingdom. I did not grow up in a Christian home nor did I know any believers. But I had a philosophy that was my own. I was convinced that God was for weak people who couldn't stand on their own two feet. God wasn't part of a thinking person's world. In fact, for me as a university student, I came kicking into the kingdom. I had to be confronted with the irrefutable words of Jesus. I had to be meet the living, reigning, saving Christ.

A Different Kind of Kingdom

As I read about the times of Jesus, there were some who wanted Him to set up an earthly kingdom. Peter was ready to do it. He even carried a sword with him to the garden of prayer. Later Peter understood. That's when he wrote, "The end of all things is near. Therefore be alert and of sober mind so that you can pray. Above all, love each other deeply, because love covers over a multitude of sins." Then Peter added, "If anyone speaks, they should do so as one who speaks the very words of God…so that in all things God may be praised through Jesus Christ" (1 Pet. 4:7–11). To reach this point, Peter must have already unpacked the Good News from what he at first had wanted it to be in order to be part of what Jesus really came to establish.

When the apostle Paul went into a pagan world with the Gospel of Christ, he was misunderstood, he was thrown into prison and he was beaten; but a young church was born that took the Gospel far and wide throughout the known world.

The early disciples were not Pharisees or Sadducees or followers of Caesar. They were followers of Jesus; they were known as people of the Way. John wrote to us: "Dear children, let us not love with words or speech but with actions and in truth" (1 John 3:18). That's what a follower of the Way does. He doesn't clutter up the way or the truth.

With Action and with Truth

Did the early Christians always agree with each other? No. If they had, we might not have the epistles because those epistles deal with a lot of disagreements and problems among the early Christians.

God has placed us here, at this time in this place, as His witnesses. We have a clear message of redemption to proclaim. We want people to hear that message. I try to stay focused on Jesus. And when I go to someone who is without the Savior, I go thinking about being an ambassador for Jesus. I want to have no other agenda.

I've been reading the prophet Ezekiel and what he wrote in Ezekiel 34:11–15. He wrote what God said: "I myself will search for my sheep and look after them. As a shepherd looks after his scattered flock when he is with them, so will I look after my sheep. I will rescue them from all the places where they were scattered on a day of clouds and darkness. I will pasture them...I will tend them in a good pasture... I myself will tend my sheep."

There are a lot of frightened scattered sheep out there. God wants them to come into His pasture. He wants to be their Shepherd. We can join with the Great Shepherd of the sheep and help to bring people into His sheepfold. There may be wolves and lions out there; there always have been and there always will be. But our Lord, the Lord of love and grace, is drawing people to Himself. We can help to call lost sheep to the Shepherd.

When I read Isaiah's message, I find it is uncluttered (Isaiah 55:1–9):
"Come, all you who are thirsty,
come to the waters;
and you who have no money,
come, buy and eat!
Come, buy wine and milk
without money and without cost.
Why spend money on what is not bread,
and your labor on what does not satisfy?
Listen, listen to me, and eat what is good,
and you will delight in the richest of fare.

Give ear and come to me;
listen, that you may live.
I will make an everlasting covenant with you,
my faithful love promised to David.
See, I have made him a witness to the peoples,
a ruler and commander of the peoples.
Surely you will summon nations you know not,
and nations you do not know will come running to you,
because of the LORD your God,
the Holy One of Israel,
for he has endowed you with splendor."
Seek the LORD while he may be found;
call on him while he is near.
Let the wicked forsake their ways
and the unrighteous their thoughts.
Let them turn to the LORD, and he will have mercy on them,
and to our God, for he will freely pardon.
"For my thoughts are not your thoughts,
neither are your ways my ways,"
declares the LORD.
"As the heavens are higher than the earth,
so are my ways higher than your ways
and my thoughts than your thoughts."

That's a straightforward and uncluttered message; that's to be our message too. We go to a person with God's Good News. We are sent and guided by the Holy Spirit. We are not out to win a political argument. We can win an argument and lose the person. We want that person to come to saving faith.

The Great Disconnect

Christians used to be known as a people of the Scriptures, followers of biblical truth. We aren't known that way anymore.

In a discussion about religion, a man who is a secular intellectual, whose good mind I respect, said, "I could never become a Christian." He went on to say "When I read the New Testament teachings of Jesus and then listen to evangelical Christians, I see a great disconnect." I couldn't disagree with him because I am seeing the same disconnect. What is so troubling is that he did not say anything in opposition to Jesus. He is opposed not to Jesus but to those who call themselves followers of Jesus.

The apostle Paul was able to say, "When I came to you, I did not come with eloquence or human wisdom as I proclaimed to you the testimony about God. For I resolved to know nothing while I was with you except Jesus Christ and him crucified. I came to you in weakness with great fear and trembling. My message and my preaching were not with wise and persuasive words, but with a demonstration of the Spirit's power, so that your faith might not rest on human wisdom, but on God's power" (1 Cor. 2:1–5). Do I have that same determination? Or, do I substitute man's wisdom, man's agenda, man's goals for the message of Jesus Christ and Him crucified?

Do We Still Believe God?

Have I yielded my will and my wants to God's perfect will or to something else? Do I trust God or do I have to make things happen in my way and in my time? Can I allow God to work His plan or must God move according to my plan?

When I listen to professed Bible-believing Christians who have a platform and are usually the ones interviewed by the media, I hear little Gospel or biblical teaching. Instead I hear them talking about all their add-ons to the Gospel. One day, after listening to a brother passionately talking about all that he believed about our failings as a country and our government leaders and what we needed to do about it, I finally asked him, "Don't you believe in God anymore?"

He thinks that he is applying the Bible to life. But since much of what he is saying is based not on Bible truth but on the media propaganda he has come to believe, he is adding lies to the truths about the saving work of Jesus. It appears that he doesn't believe the teachings of Scripture anymore. And the culture hears our substitute teachings loud and clear.

I find myself asking my Christian brothers and sisters, "If all the people around us do what you want; if they all come to your political position, will they then be Christians? If they agree with each and every one of your concerns for the culture, and pornography is eliminated and no one ever has an abortion and homosexuals are no longer militant and children don't have violent video games to watch and marriage is considered sacred, would we then have a Christian society?"

If so, then we no longer need the One sent by God for our salvation. It would no longer be necessary to trust in Christ. We would be saved by living "correctly" and placing the correct political party in power. Never mind that the Bible teaches that we are saved by faith, not by works. In fact the truth is, "…he saved us, not because of righteous things we had done, but because of his mercy" (Titus 3:5).

But that's not what so many of us are proclaiming to our needy world. They hear us proclaiming other saving means. And, when our hearers reject those other means of salvation that they hear us offering, we think they are rejecting Jesus. We have set up our doctrine of Christian morality as though we can be moral Christians on our own without the total change that comes from the new birth. When we do that, we have presented a false message to a spiritually hungry people and then we wonder why people don't want what we offer.

So we denounce them, call them pagans, announce that the nation is going to the devil while all the time we are alienating them through our cluttered-faith proclamation that is not a true proclamation of faith at all. It has left out the One who came to seek and to save that which was lost and instead has added teaching that can never save.

We have cluttered our Gospel. We have walked away from the One who saves and have substituted our own ideas, concepts, rules, and then assumed that if people will only accept our political and social ideas, they too will be Christians. They won't be.

chapter 2

What They See Is What They Get

In my work as editor of *Decision* magazine, I had the privilege of traveling the world with Billy Graham. I remember an evangelistic series of meetings in the northern part of Europe where some people paraded outside the stadium carrying signs that read, "Give Christians Power and They Will Kill You."

I thought, well, these are extremists who just don't have any idea of what Christianity is all about. They haven't heard about the Prince of Peace, the One who taught, "You shall love your neighbor as yourself."

But a few months later we were in a Midwestern city in the United States. Mr. Graham was holding a press conference. A young reporter stood up to ask a question. He wasn't belligerent; in fact, he was rather hesitant. He said, "Mr. Graham, you have come here because you want more people to become Christians. If more people do become Christians, will other people be safe on the streets?"

Where could he have gotten such an idea, such a fear of Christians? He didn't get it from reading the Bible. There was only one way—he had been watching Christians.

The Christians he saw, even in such a family-oriented, conservative part of our country, were not reflective of the Christ revealed in Scripture. He saw a Christian faith that was hurtful even dangerous to others.

If I am going to unpack the Gospel, if I am going to strip away everything that has buried the truth that I am trying to proclaim, then I have to see that what I have added to Jesus are the very things that are off-putting to others. We think they have rejected the Savior. How will we know that if what they are rejecting right now is all the stuff that we have added to Jesus? Maybe the Holy Spirit is at work in people's lives and they want what God offers in the saving Christ, but we have placed so many impediments in their way that instead of making the rough places smoother and the valleys level many of us have made the rough places rougher and the valleys deeper.

Adversarial Christians

So many vocal Christians seem to have decided that we are at war. We need enemies. We are good people; other people are evil. We have to stop those who would destroy us. We feel threatened and have to respond to the threat. We have to protect God. These are easy conclusions to come to once we have taken our eyes off God and put them squarely on our culture and those in the culture who do not behave as we think they should. As one reporter wrote, "Holy warriors need demonic enemies."

So we look for those enemies in our midst. There seems to be a built-in need to find conspiracies around us. Soon we are saying things that are not true but, we conclude, they must be true because we have already decided that we are fighters for God and we must fight all others who are evil people. Adolf Hitler had a similar view. The Jews, the Communists, were everywhere and they were out to destroy Germany. He was a maniac, of course.

We have our assumed "death panels" and "gun registries" to fight against. Neither is true, but once brought up to play on people's fears they have taken on a life of their own. Those who love secret agendas are always fair game for someone else who wants to frighten them into reacting the "correct" way. Sometimes all it takes for some Christians to go off on a frightened rampage is a mere suggestion of evil; then quickly that suggestion becomes a fact, especially for those who want to hear about conspiracies, hidden agendas and secret actions. And the last thing most Christians will do is to check to see if there is any truth to what is causing them such fear. They seem to like the fear.

When Frank Porter Stansberry released his video "End of America," he added to people's conspiracy fears. He warned of a major collapse in America and said life in America as we have known it will cease to exist. The fear for America and for his family that he speaks about fits with what so many Christians fear. And many Christians believed him. What he doesn't mention to his Christian followers is the 1.5 million dollar penalty fine that he paid in 2007 for security fraud. It is enough for some Christians that he is telling them what they already want to hear.

In his fiction book, *Paris,* Edward Rutherfurd has the Vicomte de Cygne explaining to his son: "If we can see a conspiracy, then it's proved. If we can't see it, then the conspirators must be hiding it. This is a logic from which there is no escape." For many Christians, fiction has become nonfiction.

If we refuse to join with the conspiracy-minded Christians and instead turn to Scripture, if we try to be obedient to Jesus, we are almost seen as traitors because, we are told, we are apparently blind to what is going on around us. Never mind that many followers of Jesus have looked very carefully at what is going on around us and have recognized that some Christians who think they are fighting against evil are contributing to it instead.

Those who want to follow Jesus on His terms instead of their own human terms no longer seem to fit either in the world or in the evangelical church. It is sometimes a lonely place to be when we have to try to explain to unbelievers the behavior of

Christians who are sometimes as hateful as those they see in the world, because then we also have to explain to our fellow believers that darkness cannot pretend to be light. We are to be the light bringers. We try to walk faithfully, always ready to give a reason for the hope that is in us. It is a hope based on who Jesus is, not in building our lives on our anger at the conspiracies we look for in the people who live around us.

The Culture Is Watching

It was a sad moment for me when a person who already said very plainly that he was not a Christian asked me a simple question. His question was, "Why don't Christians follow their Founder?"

Should I have answered, "We do follow our Founder"? Is what he sees in us really what we want him to understand about what it means to follow the Savior? Is the message from us that is seen and heard by so many in the culture based on God's teaching and the example of Jesus? Or is that man seeing something quite different. If I were to say, "We are following our Founder," would I send him even farther away since what he is seeing and hearing from many of us is not of Jesus at all? We used to be known as people of biblical faith. I don't find that we are known that way anymore.

The apostle Peter spoke about believers being criticized. He said that we who follow Jesus are aliens and strangers in our world. We are to live such lives among those who are unbelievers that even though they criticize us it is for living good lives. When others can rightfully criticize us for speaking about Jesus with our tongues while by our actions we are busy making Jesus our own political pawn, then we have earned the criticism we deserve.

What the world sees in us is what the world gets from us. But we as followers of Jesus don't have to be that way. When will change come? When will revival come and biblical values once again be taught and observed by the followers of Jesus?

We read in Colossians 1:22 that Christ through His death presents us "holy in his sight, without blemish and free from accusation." Why aren't people seeing that in us? Is it because the rest of that passage, (verse 23) is not being obeyed? It reads, "...if you continue in your faith, established and firm, not moved from the hope held out in the gospel." Is that why that man could ask me, "Why don't Christians follow their Founder"?

Why Must the Culture Make Christians Feel Comfortable?

Naghmeh Abedini, wife of Pastor Saeed Abedini who was sent to an Iranian prison for preaching the Gospel, has a word for her fellow believers about suffering. In a September 2013 *Decision* magazine interview she said, "[God] has caused me to embrace the suffering, rather than run from it. In the Western culture, we are taught to isolate ourselves from trials and adversity...I say embrace it."

As followers of the Christ who suffered brutally and died for us, do we try to escape persecution and harm? Do we recognize that the believer in Jesus is not going to fit in comfortably with the surrounding culture? Many Christians seem to think that the culture has an obligation to make Christians comfortable. Does the Bible read, "For God did not send his Son into the world to condemn the world, but to save the word through him"—*and to make sure that life will be comfortable for American Christians* (John 3:17)?

When did it become a Christian belief that the secular world, the unsaved culture, is obliged to make Christians comfortable? Where does Scripture teach that, as followers of Jesus, we are called to be cared for and coddled, with nothing occurring in our society that is upsetting to us?

The apostle John understood what so many of us have forgotten. When he was in exile, on the island of Patmos, he wrote a letter to the seven churches that we can read in the Book of Revelation (see Revelation 1:4 & 9). He told them that he was their partner in the tribulation and the kingdom. Somehow, today, we have come to believe that we are to enjoy all of the blessings of the kingdom but experience none of the tribulation caused by others. Either we don't read our Bibles very well or we have chosen to ignore the parts that don't tell us what we want to hear. Also, we seem to have forgotten the stories of those faithful Christians who went through tribulation throughout church history.

As I listen to Christians berate the fallen nature of the people in the culture around us, it is usually with an expression of shock. And it is always caused by "them." There is "us" and there is "them," and it is "them" who don't behave the way we think they should behave.

I hear the rants against "them" as though it is somehow possible for darkness to behave as light. Why are we blaming darkness for being dark? How can darkness behave as light? Darkness can behave only as darkness. We might want darkness to pretend to be light in order not to upset us, but darkness can't do it.

The apostle Paul reminds us that "He has rescued us from the dominion of darkness (Col. 1:13). Can the rescued criticize those who have not yet been rescued? God has qualified us to share in the inheritance of the saints in the kingdom of light (see Colossians 1:12). God did this for us; we couldn't bring ourselves into the kingdom of light and neither can anyone else. We who have been delivered from the dominion of darkness can't be critical of those who are not yet delivered. We could not deliver ourselves; neither can they.

I find Christians acting as though they are shocked at the way unbelievers behave. Why is this shocking? Remember the early church and the culture it was in? Look at the words of the apostle Peter. He could have written these words this morning:

...the Lord knows how to rescue the godly from trials and to hold the unrighteous for punishment on the Day of Judgment. This is especially true of those who follow the corrupt desire of the flesh and despise authority.

Bold and arrogant, they are not afraid to heap abuse on celestial beings; yet even angels, although they are stronger and more powerful, do not heap abuse on such beings when bringing judgment on them from the Lord. But these people blaspheme in matters they do not understand. They are like unreasoning animals, creatures of instinct, born only to be caught and destroyed, and like animals they too will perish.

They will be paid back with harm for the harm they have done. Their idea of pleasure is to carouse in broad daylight. They are blots and blemishes, reveling in their pleasures while they feast with you. With eyes full of adultery, they never stop sinning; they seduce the unstable; they are experts in greed—an accursed brood! They have left the straight way and wandered off to follow the way of Balaam son of Bezer, who loved the wages of wickedness. But he was rebuked for his wrongdoing by a donkey—an animal without speech—who spoke with a human voice and restrained the prophet's madness.

These people are springs without water and mists driven by a storm. Blackest darkness is reserved for them (2 Pet. 2:9–17).

Having read what Peter wrote, we also read that his biggest concern was not that the culture behaved that way but that believers would be tempted to do the same. Look at verse 20: "For if, after they have escaped the defilements of the world through the knowledge of our Lord and Savior Jesus Christ, they are again entangled in them and overcome, the last state has become worse for them than the first."

Didn't Jesus say to His followers, "You are the light of the world..." (Matt. 5:14)? We who belong to the Light are called to be bearers of that light to a dark world. We are to "Put the light on a lampstand…" What we are never to do, said Jesus, is to hide that light under a bushel or a bowl. Yet that is exactly what so many Christians are doing. The people around us can no longer see the light; they see only the bushel basket. We have covered the light with political hate speech, angry denunciations and disgust with the world around us. And the culture we live in hears us loud and clear. So then we are asked what that man asked me: "Why don't Christians follow their Founder?"

Sharia Christians

One day each week I meet with a group of thinking individuals who explore ideas, current events and other issues of the day. Every now and again someone will speak in a derogatory manner about "the religionists." Explore that with them and they conclude that most problems in the world are caused by religious people and therefore the world would be a better place if Christians, Muslims and other religious people would be silent and mind their own business while other people try to accomplish good in our world. As one man stated, "We live in a secular world. But now we have religious fanatics who strap bombs to their bodies and feel they will go to heaven." There is fear of guns in the hands of the Taliban in Afghanistan and fear of guns in the hands of right-wing Christians in America. Both are seen as dangerous religious fanatics.

Just as so many secular people fear the dogmatic, angry teaching of Sharia-law Muslims, they fear Christians who want to impose their Christian version of Sharia law on our country. They think that's what we are trying to do because that's the way we sound to them. They don't know from us that there is a Savior who alone changes hearts and brings people to new life.

One Christian speaks to another. They agree on so much that they assume any thinking person would feel the same as they do.

It never occurs to them that others in need of the Good News are not thinking that same way at all. Neither does it occur to many Christians that what others see in us sends them running the other way. Do they run from us because of our biblical faithfulness? Is it because we follow Jesus? We'd like to think so, but if we thought that we'd mostly be wrong. It isn't usually our biblical truth that drives so many unbelievers away, it is our lives and the lies they see us following. They see and hear those lies and react to them. Lying seems to have become a Christian virtue, as we will see in chapter three.

It is true that the apostle Paul tells us, "The person without the Spirit does not accept the things that come from the Spirit of God but considers them foolishness, and cannot understand them because they are discerned only through the Spirit" (1 Cor. 2:14). Do the unbelievers fear us because we know Gospel truth or do they fear us and avoid us for other reasons entirely? Is it that they do not see the Spirit in us but only political and social anger that makes us seem to be haters of other people?

In his letter to Titus, the apostle Paul reminds us of the way we all were before meeting the Savior: "At one time we too were foolish, disobedient, deceived and enslaved by all kinds of passions and pleasures. We lived in malice and envy, being hated and hating one another" (Titus 3:3). That is the way we used to be. That isn't the way we are to behave now if we are living in Christ.

But either we have forgotten this or we ourselves have never really been changed by the new birth and we are showing the culture that Jesus doesn't really make any difference in a person's life. When James in his epistle spoke of faith and works, it is obvious that the one follows the other. But people can't see our faith, no matter how much we speak of it, if what they are seeing is what we do in the name of Jesus that does not demonstrate who Jesus is.

The apostle Paul continued by giving us a ringing reminder: "But when the kindness and love of God our Savior appeared, he saved us, not because of righteous things we had done, but because of his mercy" (Titus 3:4–5). Are we living out those words in our world? When we were welcomed by the Savior it was not because of our righteous works. How then can we expect those without the Savior to have righteous works? And even if they could, would that change their hearts and lives or is it by God's mercy that we are a delivered people? Intentionally or not, we continue to tell others who haven't yet come to faith, "You have to behave like Christians, while I, who profess faith in Christ, do not." What the world sees in us is what they get from us—and too often it is hypocrisy.

Toward the conclusion of that rich chapter three in the epistle to Titus, Paul wrote, "But avoid foolish controversies and genealogies and arguments and quarrels about the law, because they are unprofitable and useless." Then, describing some of the people in the church, the apostle wrote that such a person is "…warped and sinful; they are self-condemned" (Titus 3:9–11). The world doesn't listen to people who are warped and sinful and self-condemned.

Blind to People's Emptiness

In her book *Gravity and Grace,* Simone Weil said, "Every sin is an attempt to fly from emptiness." Are we so busy checking out the sin in our world that we miss the emptiness behind it? How is it that we have become so worked up about attacking sin that we have forgotten why sin is there in the first place?

Certainly we see around us a sinning people. But what they do isn't what makes them sinners. All of us sin because by nature we already are sinners. And if, by some means, we could avoid sinning, our nature would still not have changed until God changes it. That's why it is so wrong to try to make unredeemed people act like redeemed people so that we will be more comfortable and won't have to experience the results of their sin. They can't be what they are not without first experiencing the redemptive work of Christ in their lives.

But instead of recognizing who people are, what they face and the emptiness they are trying to flee, we make them angry with our accusations and condemnation. This is like expecting a left-handed pitcher to throw right-handed strikes and then making him frustrated and angry by our expectations of him.

The world sees us and hears us. The people who watch us fear us, for in their eyes we have become so strident, so angry, that we will take stands that are not biblical, follow teachings that never came from Jesus, while calling ourselves followers of the truth. No wonder the world rejects us and our "truth." They no longer see Christ in us.

Little Difference between Islam and Christianity

Jonathan Haidt, who writes and teaches about social and moral psychology, noticed what happened following the attacks on the Twin Towers and the Pentagon on 9/11. He said in his book *The Righteous Mind*, "…some scientists saw little distinction between Islam and Christianity. All religions, they said, are delusions that prevent people from embracing science, secularism, and modernity. The horror of 9/11 motivated several of these scientists to write books, and between 2004 and 2007 so many such books were published that a movement was born. It was called, "The New Atheism."

To people like the outspoken Richard Dawkins, religion is antifact, a fantasy, and promotes hostility in the world. So when he and others of like mind listen to Christians who often sound to them as just as hateful as extremist Muslims and who demand that the country follow Christian behavior and laws, we who are followers of Jesus play right into their hands. We confirm what they already believe about us. The sad part is that we are confirming what they believe about Christians by everything we do that isn't Christian.

A Canadian journalist friend, who always writes thoughtful pieces, wrote an article based on an interview he saw in the *United Church Observer*. He picked up the words, "You always have to have an enemy" and, illustrating his own view, said, "…politics sometimes turns otherwise gentle people into vessels of vitriol. It is part of the adversarial system."

My friend wasn't writing about Christians and politics in the United States. For many years he has held credentials that allow him to observe and write about what happens in Parliament in Ottawa, Canada. But, as a sound believer, he sees what adversarial anger can do. I think we are on the same page about this even though we are in different countries living under different political systems. We serve the same Lord and see the same problems when Christian behavior is not Christian.

Our Cut-Down Version of the Bible

When the apostle Paul wrote to Titus, he told him, "Remind the people to be subject to rulers and authorities, to be obedient, to be ready to do whatever is good, to slander no one, to be peaceable and considerate, and always to be gentle toward everyone" (Titus 3:1–2). Does the world see us behaving like that? Or does the world see us doing the opposite? Does Paul anywhere tell us to act and think as the world acts and thinks? Don't we read in Colossians 1:10 that we are to "…live a life worthy of the Lord and please him in every way: bearing fruit in every good work"?

Apparently many of us have cut those words out of our Bibles. Or, we have come to believe that fighting and accusations, especially false political accusations that are heard on the lips of so many vocal and strident Christians, are acceptable behavior. Do we believe that we no longer have to obey God's word because the statement, "All Scripture is God-breathed and is useful for teaching, rebuking, correcting and training in righteousness, so that the servant of God may be thoroughly equipped for every good work" (2 Tim. 3:16–17) is no longer true for us? Or do we assume that we can give lip service to it but, in certain areas of life, we no longer have to practice it? Or do we assume that those scriptural words do not apply to teaching us, correcting us, rebuking us, and training us in righteousness? The world is watching us.

Called to Dominate?

Are we "dominists"? The Bible tells us that when man was created by God, we were to "Be fruitful and increase in number; fill the earth and subdue it. Rule over the fish in the sea and the birds in the sky and over every living creature that moves on the ground" (Gen. 1:28). There are those who teach that just as believers are to have dominion over the earth, believers are mandated biblically to control or occupy politics and the political institutions until Christ returns. We are to be active in politics and dominate the political process. Some day we will rule with Christ; therefore, say some Christians, we are to dominate and rule here now.

But are we ruling with God now? Is the kingdom of God here in the United States of America now and therefore God expects us to reform, change, vote out and vote in so that the kingdom will be made right for us now? Or is this one more thing that we have added to our biblical teaching in order to justify our attempts at changing political systems in our own country and elsewhere? Did the early disciples try to do that? Were the political and cultural systems they lived under suited to them, functioning the way they wanted them to function? Or did they learn how to go into their world with the message of the life-changing, redeeming Christ, relying on the Holy Spirit to guide and help them no matter what political system they were under?

Filling Our Minds with Anger

There is a reason that Christians are often seen by those around us as unloving and adversarial. Too many believers have become followers of those who aren't Christians, who don't obey Scripture but who are adversarial and angry. We have filled our minds with what they teach without even realizing what we are doing.

Fewer people, including Christians, want to think of themselves as moderates or centrists, people of a cooperative middle way. The idea of compromising in life sounds like we are compromising biblical truth. Moderation isn't always seen as an admirable quality anymore. In earlier days in the United States, it was the moderates or centrists who were able to work together and get things done. Now we are fragmented, divisive, with one person ready to attack another person the moment he suggests that we might be able to get along. And often Christians are right in the middle of it. We sharpen our spears and prepare to defend our tribe against that other tribe—those evil people known as "them."

We have become known for the very thing we are warned against by James in his epistle. The apostle tells us in chapter four, "You quarrel and fight." He speaks of becoming friends not of God but of the world. When we unite with the world over political fracturing are we behaving as friends or enemies of God? James says we are enemies of God. Our politicized gospel is taking on battles in the world and with the world and withholding from other people the clear saving message of Christ. We are no longer doing what Jesus told us to do when He ascended into heaven. We have substituted anger for love, our politics for His kingship and our social demands for God's invitation.

Those Ever-present Emails

Andrea and I have several Christian friends who are very right-wing ultra-conservative Christians. They are good people and good friends. They send us emails. These are blanket emails spread far and wide to the people on their contact list. They not only send them to everyone they know, they urge us to pass them on to the people we know because Christians have to band together to save America from the evil people who are trying to destroy our country.

Even though I understand their passion, would an unsaved person understand what these Christians are saying and be confused about what the Christian message really is? How would an unsaved person think about Jesus and the Christian faith if he received one of those blanket emails?

Prior to the 2008 presidential election in which Barack Obama was first elected, when candidates were still in the primary stage, we were receiving hateful emails about Senator John McCain. To these conservative Christian friends sending us those emails (who were for other candidates in the primary race), John McCain was not just wrong in his political views; he was evil, demonic, of the devil. The country would not be worth living in if he were to be elected.

But then McCain became the candidate on the Republican side and Barack Obama became the candidate on the Democratic side. The email senders switched their focus without changing their wording. John McCain was suddenly "baptized." He was the Christian's candidate, the man God wanted in office. The emails sent to us said that we Christians had to make sure that John McCain was elected if we wanted a country worth living in.

Now Barack Obama was seen as the one who was of the devil. In fact, comparing email with email, the exact same words that were used earlier to describe John McCain were now being used to describe Barack Obama. Only the name was changed. The writers only had to cross out one name and insert the other.

I began to wonder how non-Christians were hearing this. It isn't that candidates are on one side of a political issue or another; to these ultra-angry Christians they are either God's candidate or Satan's candidate.

Is Being Right in Our Politics the Same as Being Right with God?

It is hard for us when other Christians force us into that angry adversarial box when we don't want to be there. The world sees us all as one. For the rest of us, those vocal Christians have set up a non-Christian situation. We are seen as people who have exchanged Christ and His church for particular political stands. But being on the right side politically doesn't make a person right with God. Only the saving work of Jesus can do that. The apostle Peter reminds us, "Through him you believe in God, who raised him from the dead and glorified him, and so your faith and hope are in God (1 Pet. 1:21). Through Him, not through a political party or laws passed or some media personality who is followed and quoted by the Christians. God the Father raised Jesus from the dead. The Father glorified Him, not anything or anyone else. Our faith and our hope are centered in God. How can the redeemed forget who redeemed them?

Suppose I had gone to a person to talk to him about Jesus and he said, "Oh yes, I'm a Christian. I'm voting for John McCain. He is God's candidate. I'm following God's will. I certainly want to be on God's side."

I'd have to bring a person like this to the same point as the person who thinks that his church membership or something else will save him. I'd have to try to undo what the vocal political Christians had taught him and try to help him see the one-and-only Savior. Jesus saves; no one is saved by how he votes.

Or, the opposite could take place, "Don't talk to me about your Jesus. I don't like John McCain and I won't vote for him. If he is the candidate of your Christian God, then I have no interest in your God."

I find that the best thing to do in this situation is to acknowledge that, "Yes, some Christians are saying that. But no one speaks for God unless he is saying what God has given to us in His word."

There is a more basic need that all of us have. Jesus said, "I am the way and the truth and the life. No one comes to the Father except through me" (John 14:6). Or, look at Peter's words, "Salvation is found in no one else, for there is no other name under heaven given to mankind by which we must be saved" (Acts. 4:12). Being angry with others, trying to change the voting of others, attempting to make the country more Godlike, can't be done by venting our disgust with other people. There is only one Savior and He isn't our favorite politician. Yet we keep telling the culture that our favorite politician is the country's savior.

We seem to want people to make our surroundings more like a little bit of heaven. But no one can do that. The unbelievers upset us by their behavior as if God is not aware of their behavior and, more importantly, aware of their need. He sent His Son to this world because God so loved the world. Have Christians stopped believing that? Is anger and political preaching our only way to respond to those who are lost? Jesus didn't teach that.

There is no point in defending the angry statements of some Christians. I can only say to my wounded unsaved friends, "I don't find Jesus teaching that and I am trying to be a follower of Jesus."

Learning about Hateful Christians

Unfortunately, the culture already knows about hateful Christians. It is the Christians who don't realize what message they are communicating. It isn't the message of Jesus.

How do we present our Christian message so that it is heard? What Scripture will lift people to a higher plane so that they only see Jesus and why He came to die for us and why He rose again for us?

I find myself saying things like, "Certainly that person has a right to her personal views." Then I add, "Even if every person voted the way I would like him to vote, that wouldn't make us a Christian country? If every law was written to suit me, we would still be a lost people in need of the Savior?" And then I try to bring a person back to what really matters, the condition of his eternal soul.

I assure whoever I am talking to that we all are in need of the saving work of Christ. This is a message that needs to be told, but it needs to be told without reinforcing what the culture sees in a people who call themselves Christians but who give no evidence that they are trying to follow the Prince of Peace.

When I look into Scripture and see words such as those written in Ephesians 2, I wonder why we have added so much clutter to the Gospel, why we have become known not as followers of Jesus but as followers of a political party or some social agenda. What happened to our understanding of, "For it is by grace you have been saved, through faith—and this is not from yourselves, it is the gift of God—not by works, so that no one can boast" (Eph. 2:8–9)?

The apostle continues with the words, "For we are God's handiwork, created in Christ Jesus to do good works, which God prepared in advance for us to do." Is it the message of salvation by faith through grace or is it something totally opposite to that message that God has prepared for us to proclaim? Are the good works prepared in advance for us to do political or social works that are something other than those taught by Jesus and His saving work?

Anger and hatred can give people a feeling of power and smug superiority. But neither of those are marks of a true believer. When we begin to relish our self-empowerment, we bring added clutter to the Gospel. The ones who need to understand the Gospel have become lost in that clutter, lost to the hope we can share in Christ, lost to the light, and lost to all the good that has been done by followers of Jesus in the past.

In our new Christian view, is what Jesus said about Himself and why He came no longer true? Have we substituted our social and political preferences for God's truth? Would a Christian knowingly twist God's truth as a means to present his own version of truth? Wouldn't that be lying? Too many Christians seem to be doing it.

chapter 3

Lying: A Christian Virtue?

I was teaching in an evangelical theological seminary in the south. The students were Doctor of Ministry candidates and I was teaching a J-term course on "Expanding Your Ministry through Writing."

One day, as we were discussing journalism ethics, I mentioned a publication that had left the Evangelical Press Association when I was a board member of that organization. The editor of that magazine was publishing false information, untruths, when our code of ethics called for fair and balanced reporting. The editor had signed that code. When the board asked him to honor the code, he refused and, in order to not have to stop what he was doing, pulled his publication out of the Evangelical Press Association.

I told that story to the class but did not mention the name of the publication. I found that I didn't have to. The class members named that publication immediately and told me that most of them were readers of that magazine and were pleased that the editor had the gumption not to be limited by the ethical code of the Evangelical Press Association. "But he is lying in print," I explained. Those evangelical pastors then let me know in very blunt terms that as far as they were concerned, "It is okay to lie as long as we are lying for Jesus."

Is it okay to lie? Is that a new Christian stance that is permissible in our age when "everyone else lies"? With those pastors all I could do was refer to the words of the apostle Peter who said, "For we did not follow cleverly devised stories when we told you about the coming of our Lord Jesus Christ in power, but we were eyewitnesses of his majesty" (2 Pet. 1:16).

According to Scripture, Christians don't lie. We faithfully tell the truth; we do not use cleverly invented stories even if we think we are doing it to help our cause, be it social, political or religious. Otherwise, we are not only liars but we are hypocrites, doing the very thing that Scripture warns us not to do while all the time insisting that we are obedient followers of God's word.

The apostle Paul stated what should be descriptive of believers: "...we have renounced secret and shameful ways; we do not use deception, nor do we distort the word of God" (2 Cor. 4:2). Can those who support "lying for Jesus" read these words without blushing?

Transforming Our Political Discourse

Who is worse, the politician or newscaster who tells lies or the Christian who repeats those lies to others? Who will be more accountable to God, the secular person who doesn't know any better or the professed follower of Jesus who does?

I wonder what would happen in our culture if the Christians decided that they would repeat information only after they checked it for accuracy. I wonder what changes would come if believers in Jesus thought first of what is best for other people and less about what is good for their own political or social position. And what might happen if Christians measured their "yesses" and their "no's" based on the standards of Jesus and the teachings that He gave us?

We tend to make a "sin list" that includes the sins of other people but excludes our own. But when we look at the list of people in Scripture who are destined for the lake of fire, it is a list that is a bit different than ours. We read, "But the cowardly, the unbelieving, the vile, the murderers, the sexually immoral, those who practice magic arts, the idolaters and all liars—they will be consigned to the fiery lake of burning sulfur" (Rev. 21:8).

We may find ourselves agreeing with this Scripture until we come to that pause, that stopping for emphasis, which adds "and all liars." Am I somehow excused from being one of those in the lake of fire because I followed all but the last? If I want politics to suit me, or I don't like the evil that I see around me in my culture, am I permitted to pass along lies to promote my "Christian principles"? How do we explain that passage of Scripture to seekers? How do we explain that passage of Scripture to those who want nothing to do with us because we are seen as people who lie and who worship at the throne of those on television who feed us with the lies that we tell?

Do We Have Another Bible?

Once we were known as people of biblical truth. Now we are becoming known as people of the political lie. So we become upset, label those who disagree with us as "liberals" and show even more anger toward them. Yet we don't hear what they are saying about our inconsistency, the difference between quoting Scripture and living Scripture.

Whereas once we followed Scripture, now many have added extra-biblical teaching to our faith. Yes, we even repeat lies. I've lost count of how many times born-again people have said to me, "Rush says…," referring to radio speaker Rush Limbaugh. I don't hear these same people stating, "The Bible says…."

In spite of the fact that various radio stations and advertisers are dropping Rush Limbaugh for his incendiary statements, Limbaugh has become a source of inspiration for many Bible-believing Christians. It doesn't matter to them that he has demonstrated his bias and often limited ability as a thinker. He briefly attended Southeast Missouri State University but, according to his mother, "He flunked everything." He then managed to hurt his mind with overdoses of prescription drugs. He can't even stay married very long. But he is, for many Christians, the man to quote. Then we wonder why thinking secularists who disagree with our apparent worship of Rush Limbaugh and his teachings seem to us to be disagreeing with our Bible teaching about Jesus. It may not be our Bible teaching that they are disagreeing with. They don't agree with Limbaugh and they don't respect those of us who swear by his every word without even checking to see if what he says can be backed up by the truth. I can't ask Rush Limbaugh to not be Rush Limbaugh. He is what he is. But I can ask my brothers and sisters in Christ not to follow him as though he is an oracle from God.

When I teach writing students or when I help authors develop their books, I will often see references to events that I know are not true. I can only point the student or the author to the factual information surrounding that false story that has been told so many times it has become an urban legend. But some argue with me. They feel that what they write is true, not false, because it is about a subject or person that they already want to be angry about. And so they cannot be taught, they cannot be pointed to what is true and they will not consider that lies are lies, even when those lies are passed along to them by fellow believers.

When John, writing the book of Revelation, paused in his listing of those destined for the lake of fire and said "and all liars," we don't want to hear it. Our emotions, our anger that gives us a sense of empowerment, our hatred of a person or cause, will trump truth every time. Those who know us and listen to us wonder at the beliefs of Christians when what they hear from us is too often neither true nor Christian. Those unbelievers in our midst miss the right things by rejecting the wrong things that we have tried to propagate. How many lost people will we be responsible for when, instead of pointing to Jesus, we point to the sayings of Rush Limbaugh or Bill O'Reilly or Glenn Beck? So many well-meaning believers do not even realize that what they are saying or doing is hurting the very message of Jesus they so desperately want others to hear. We are driving people away from the Savior.

Why Would He Say That?

One day I read statements about President Obama made by Christian singer Pat Boone. In his "The President Without a Country" statement, Pat Boone "quoted" the president as saying, "We're no longer a Christian nation" and "You might say that America is a Muslim nation."

So I checked to find out what the president really said. Here are those quotes as they circulated on YouTube: "Whatever we once were, we're no longer a Christian nation. At least not just. We are also a Jewish nation, a Muslim nation, and a Buddhist nation, and a Hindu nation, and a nation of nonbelievers." So these are the words picked up by those like Pat Boone who then edited the YouTube version and restated them.

Here is what the President did say during a press conference in Turkey: "One of the great strengths of the United States is…we have a very large Christian population—we do not consider ourselves a Christian nation or a Jewish nation or a Muslim nation. We consider ourselves a nation of citizens who are bound by ideals and a set of values."

Why would Pat Boone twist a statement like that? If he wanted to attack the president, why not just quote what he actually said? Why would he arrange those words to make them say what wasn't true?

I wonder, too, if Pat knows that our first president, George Washington, in a note to Muslims in Tripoli, wrote, "As the government of the United States of America is not in any sense founded on the Christian religion…" In Article 11 of the Treaty of Tripoli that followed, these words were included without debate or change and were signed by President John Adams after being unanimously ratified by the Senate.

Our Selective Hearing

One day I heard a report on Christian radio about the president's faith. Apparently there are many Christians who don't listen to Christian radio because when I repeat to others what I heard, the immediate response is "No, that has to be a lie." Just to be certain I got a printed copy. It read: "President Barack Obama says he's a 'Christian by choice.' He said, 'My mother was one of the most spiritual people I knew, but she didn't raise me in the church… I became a Christian as an adult.' He said the precepts of Jesus Christ spoke to him, and he came to believe that Jesus died for his sins. Obama discussed his faith in response to a question. The president said he believes salvation is by God's grace. Obama said he prays daily and views his public service as an expression of his Christian faith." Then the report added, "A recent Pew Forum poll found that many Americans believe Obama is a Muslim" (Faith Report, Wednesday, September 29, 2010).

But Does the President Go To Church?

Church attendance is important for Christians and they want to see their presidents worshiping in church. Ronald Reagan rarely did, Richard Nixon didn't either, except in the East Room of the White House, but they were never criticized for it. Jimmy Carter not only attended regularly but taught a Sunday school class as well. Bill Clinton went to church but was known as a hypocrite for his later behavior with Monica Lewinsky.

What about the Obamas who were criticized for being "Muslims" at the same time they were being criticized for attending the wrong church—the Reverend Jeremiah Wright scandal. No one seemed to notice the contradiction. A person can't at the same time be criticized for being a Muslim and for being the wrong kind of Christian who attends the wrong kind of church.

The Obamas attended various churches in Washington DC, although it hurt the president when so many visitors and sightseers crowded the churches where he went to worship that the regular church members couldn't get in. The disturbance caused by his attendance as well as the Secret Service taking over the church was too much. So, according to an article in *TIME* magazine, he told his staff that "...he will follow in George W. Bush's footsteps and make his primary place of worship Evergreen Chapel, the nondenominational church at Camp David." The pastor is a Southern Baptist military chaplain.

And, in need of prayer and Christian counsel, the president has a group he calls on or who come together to pray with him. Two of them had the same role with President George W. Bush, Kirbyjon Caldwell and T.D. Jakes. One denominational leader said, "You wouldn't expect him to isolate himself spiritually. This is a man with a faith center; we've heard him give his testimony."

Yet, so many Christians want to keep blasting the president, mixing up their desire to be critical of his policies with his spiritual stand. James Dobson went on radio to say that the president was "...deliberately distorting the traditional understanding of the Bible to fit his own worldview, his own confused theology."

What Is Christian and What Is Not?

Such statements about Christianity and politics are confusing to the secular person. In South Carolina, when Richard Cash challenged Lindsey Graham for his Senate seat he said, "It is time for a new voice in Washington. We need a voice that represents Christian, conservative, and Republican principles instead of the latest bi-partisan 'deal' that makes matters worse."

How should we take such a statement? Is conservative and Republican the same as Christian? Does Christian mean a person is not bipartisan when he serves in public office? Was Lindsey Graham so bipartisan that his work could no longer be called Christian? How would an unbeliever read this? How would a Christian read it, especially one who wants his senator to work with others and not be obstinate or stubborn, blocking any forward movement that might be good for the country?

If I knew nothing about Jesus—why He came, what He taught, why He went to the cross and the power of His resurrection—would I know more or less about Christianity after hearing such a statement that uses "Christian," "conservative" and "Republican" in the same sentence? If I come down correctly on the last two points, would I then also be qualified to be labeled "Christian"? Would I then understand the way to heaven?

"We Are All Christians"

When the media pick up on the most outlandish statements by vocal Christians, it is assumed by the secular folks that all Christians think that way. But how can a follower of Jesus counter what other Christians are saying to the media? We can't outshout them, nor should we. We can live the life of a believer and be the kind of quiet, thoughtful Christians who are not followers of the vocal crowd. We can demonstrate that we are people of transformed minds.

In a small group where I was participating in a discussion, a man who attends a church where they seem to worship other things more than Jesus said to the group, "Well, we're all Christians here." There was an immediate uproar from many in the group yelling, "No," and "No we're not." Hearing them declare themselves to not be Christians, I was relieved. Those people know they aren't Christians. I will be able to talk with them about the Savior without having to battle the belief that "We are all Christians."

There is a lot of pride among those who boast that they are not Christians. It is a pride based on the assumption that they use their minds while Christians don't. They are free thinkers, they like to announce; Christians aren't. They are good and moral people; Christians are not.

Yet always in my conversations with this kind of thinker I know I will face another problem when I have opportunity to explain what a Christian is. Many of them have met only the vocal, angry, political Christians. They may have cried out, "No we're not," because they didn't hold to what they thought was Christian, not because they understood the saving work of Jesus. They may not have heard about the Savior because of what is announced by professing Christians who willingly tell falsehoods by adding what is not of Christ to what the message of Jesus really is.

"Tell the Truth Day"

Scripture tells us that "Righteousness exalts a nation, but sin condemns any people" (Prov. 14:34). And, we are told, "Mockers stir up a city, but the wise turn away anger (Prov. 29:8). So where do I and my Christian brothers and sisters stand with these words from God's truth? Am I still righteous when I condemn unrighteousness not with truth but with lies? Am I a disgrace when I add what is not true to what is holy and right? Are all Christians numbered among the righteous? Are all wise?

I've always been fascinated by the fact that three days after July 4, when we in America celebrate the founding of our country with all of its values, July 7 is proclaimed "National Tell the Truth Day." The people who present this day ask, "Is there some truth that you want to share?" Well, yes, there is a truth I want to share. I want to tell the truth about the Messiah.

But why do we need a National Tell the Truth Day? Does that mean we don't have to tell the truth on other days? Can we be liars on all but one day? The presenters of this day explain that their hope is that if a person tells the truth on one day, he may then tell the truth on a second day. And maybe he will tell the truth more days after that until he will always tell the truth. That's an interesting viewpoint in a country that many refer to as "Christian America." What does God say? "Thou shalt not bear false witness."

Christian Right-wing Apoplexy

A friend, an evangelist with the United Methodist Church, told me a story about Hillary Clinton. "But," he added, "It probably isn't a story that most Christians will believe."

He and a colleague had developed a faith sharing New Testament. It is a small New Testament with the words of Jesus highlighted and with explanations about how we can get right with God. I have a copy. He gave a copy to the Methodist Bishop in Arkansas back when Bill Clinton was governor of that state. The bishop later told my friend that he no longer had his copy because he had given it away. He explained that, while visiting him, Mrs. Clinton saw it, picked it up to look at it and said, "Oh, this is the perfect size to fit in my purse. Where can I get a copy?" So the Bishop replied, "Please, take that one." She thanked him and put it in her purse.

With a twinkle in his eye, the friend who told me about that incident said, "Many Christians will not believe that story because it is about Mrs. Clinton. But how many of those who don't want to believe it are themselves carrying a soul winner's New Testament in their purse or pocket?"

Our Double Standard

We who will select our truth and accept what appeals to us even when it is untrue will sometimes even lie to ourselves. The same Christians who wanted to make President Obama a supporter of Muslims give a free pass to people like Tea Party leader Grover Norquist who is married to a Palestinian Muslim woman, Samah Alrayyes Norquist. Grover Norquist, who is the founder and leader of Americans for Tax Reform and the primary promoter of the "Taxpayer Protection Pledge" that so many in Congress have signed, is seen as a true Republican.

It is also interesting that Christians who equate the Republican Party with the Christian faith and who attack Democrats for their positions on homosexuality won't acknowledge that the Republican Party has not just one but two gay caucuses. The older "Log Cabin Republicans" are the more middle-of-the-road gay, lesbian and transgender caucus. The newer "GOProud" Republicans are the Tea Party gay, lesbian and transgender group. And, in order to make sure that "GOProud" stays faithful to Tea Party agendas, Grover Norquist sits on their advisory board, a group he joined in 2010.

Norquist stated, "GOProud is an important part of the conservative movement. I am proud to join GOProud's Board of Advisors and to help in advancing their common-sense conservative agenda." One of Norquist's colleagues on the GOProud board is Margaret Hoover, who until recently served as a Fox News contributor.

But many Christians remain in denial about this, preferring to make all homosexuals Democrats, then denouncing

Democrats for their homosexual tolerance. The secular people, who do know about the two Republican homosexual caucuses, can only marvel and smile at Christians who will create their own make-believe world rather than live in the real one.

So when a Christian wants to talk to an unbeliever about the need to trust in Christ alone for salvation, that Christian already carries with him the baggage of being seen as foolish, out-of-touch, a person who is an advocate of many things that are not true.

Satan, we learn from Jesus, "…is a liar and the father of lies" (see John 8:44). Why then do some Christians insist on doing what the father of lies wants them to do? And how can we ever point to the one who is Truth if we are following the father of lies?

Checking Our Information

An evangelical friend who has a very effective ministry sends me emails. One day he sent an email about the "fact" that the Affordable Care Act is giving special exemptions to Muslims. It was an attack on Obamacare. So I did what I always do when I receive such emails—I checked it out.

There was no evidence of any such thing being included in the Affordable Care Act, nothing fitting the page number given about where this information is "hidden." Even on the site itself where this was announced there were notices that this was basically another urban legend. Yet, without reading on, without checking details, without looking at facts, my Christian friend sent out the email message urging all of us to pass it along. A lie is always more interesting than the truth.

Many congressional people who claim that Americans don't want the Affordable Care Act base their conclusion on surveys taken in their own districts. Those are districts made up mostly of people who think like that official in the first place. The districts have been gerrymandered, redrawn to include mostly people who believe the same as that congressional person, insuring that he will always be reelected. So his "surveys of the American people" are surveys of those who elected him.

It is curious to me that the people who took wider polls to prove that Obamacare was not wanted by the Americans people found that the numbers changed when those same people were asked if they approved of the Affordable Care Act. The negative put on Obamacare, making it sound like a one-man or all-government takeover, didn't generate the same feeling when the program was seen as the Affordable Care Act. It seems that many people are not aware that Obamacare, which is a negative, and the Affordable Care Act, which gets more positive responses, are the same thing. And it is rarely reported that there are a number of people who have said "No" when questioned about the Affordable Care Act but who, upon further questioning, explained that they said no because they felt the act didn't go far enough toward a one-payer system. That's rarely reported by the people who want to state how many are against the act.

What also is not acknowledged, according to *The Economist* (September 28, 2013) is "…a fierce effort has begun in the states to ruin it [The Affordable Care Act] by dissuading young people from signing up to insurance exchanges in the hope that the system collapses under the cost of covering only those who will need plenty of expensive treatment." Also what is rarely explained is that before the ACA, people without insurance, often rejected by insurance companies because they had preexisting illnesses, were getting their treatment in hospital emergency rooms paid for by the rest of society. People who cannot pay are entitled to emergency care under the "Emergency Medical Treatment and Active Labor Act" passed in 1986. So the effort to get ACA to collapse also guarantees that hospitals will continue to pass along expensive care for the uninsured to others.

Does Congress really care? It has been pointed out that Congress has its own gold-plated insurance plan. One Fox News watcher chortled, "You'll notice that Congress doesn't want Obamacare for themselves." My reply is that Congress doesn't want any plan that the rest of us have to pay for. They have subsidies that the rest of us don't get. And look at the various states where attempts are being made to keep ACA out. In Florida, members of the state legislature pay $8.00 per month for their own health insurance. These are the same leaders who, along with the governor, have not only tried to block the Affordable Care Act so people can't get it but tried to block "navigators" from coming into the state to explain the ACA program to people in the county health agencies where the poor and uninsured are treated.

In Florida, where 25 percent of the people are without health insurance, mostly due to poverty, the $8.00-per-month legislature payers also boast of at least 50 millionaires in their ranks. So the millionaire legislators who get their own subsidized premium health care at practically no cost to themselves are doing all they can to keep the poor from having the benefit of any health care at all. Do we as Christians care? Would Jesus care? Or can we separate our Christian convictions from the needs of the people who live among us?

Political Lies

The *Tampa Bay Times* fact-checking operation found that Republicans are responsible for 52 percent of the political lies that are told; the Democrats are responsible for 24 percent. Conversely, according to George Mason University's Center for Media and Public Affairs, 54 percent of Democratic statements were rated as "mostly true" or "true" as compared to just 18 percent of Republican statements. Yet many Christians insist that the Republicans are the truth-telling Christian party and the Democrats are not. Why would Christians say that? Both parties are made up of fallible human beings. Pronouncements by either one need to be checked out.

Christian people can become the kind of people who know what is authentic and what is not. We can be people who have discerning minds. For example, take the Benghazi embassy news story. I hear all kinds of statements being made and believed. Then, if we pass along to others what we hear, the secular person who looks into the background will probably reject what we say. From then on, it is hard to be taken seriously when we want to talk about our Savior.

When the Benghazi embassy attack was in the news, television reports were telling us that the congressional people doing the investigating about Benghazi said that such attacks as that one had never happened under the watch of George W. Bush. Why would they say that when it isn't true and all they had to do was check? And why would Christians repeat it?

All we have to do is look at the records. In 2002, the U.S. Consulate in Karachi, Pakistan, was attacked. Twelve were killed, 51 were injured. In 2004, the U.S. embassy in Uzbekistan was bombed, killing two and injuring 15. In 2006, armed men attacked the U.S. embassy in Syria; one diplomat died. And there were other such events in Grenada, 2007; Serbia and Yemen in 2008; in all a total of 13 attacks while George W. Bush was president.

Untruths or half-truths get reported in the media, and too many Christians quote the statements that they hear being made without checking to see if what is told or shown is really accurate. Then we are guilty of repeating false information. But many of the secular people I talk with have checked and do search for the truth. Why would they have any interest in a Christian witness to the message of Jesus when saying what is false seems to be acceptable to those same Christians?

The Anti-Christian Pentagon

When Christian conservatives started circulating information about the Pentagon's discrimination against Christians, disciplining and even court-martialing those who share their faith, that was a serious charge and it got a lot of play in the news. But what wasn't stated was the Pentagon's reply to the charge.

Pentagon spokesman Lt. Cmdr. Nate Christensen said, "The U.S. Department of Defense has never and will never single out a particular religion for persecution or prosecution." He said that the Department "…celebrates the religious diversity of our service members." But he also said that "…when religious harassment complaints are reported, commanders take action based on the gravity of the occurrence on a case-by-case basis." Evangelism is still permitted, the Pentagon states. But it is also noted that in recent years, with the plurality of religions, there has also been an increase in aggressive proselytism. That isn't limited to Christians.

Christians who spread rumors about the "anti-Christian stance" of the military are not being fair to the military nor to any Christians who want to share their faith in a clear, biblical manner, not by force or argument but by announcing the truths of the biblical Christian faith. True witnesses can be hurt by those who make sweeping statements about the military's being anti-Christian. Attempting to speak to someone about what he believes, a Christian has to be extra careful because some vocal Christians are making untrue statements about the military. Faithful Christians who want to have a Gospel witness sometimes have to go through a minefield laid by their own people.

Maybe We Are Only Gullible

Are we to be known in secular circles as people so gullible that we believe any and all propaganda that comes our way without ever looking behind it? Is it any wonder that to the secular person, "These Christians are so blind that they willingly believe in Jesus, the inspiration of the Bible and every piece of political nonsense that comes down the pike?" Try approaching a secular person with the good news of salvation when—in that person's mind—we have already demonstrated that we will eagerly accept and believe anything, no matter how far-fetched it is.

Why do Christians continue to feed their souls and their minds on that which makes them known as phonies and liars when we could follow Jesus, tell the truth and be able and willing to give a reason for the hope that is in us? Is it because of the propaganda we are fed and willingly believe? Weak as we are, we don't have to willfully, knowingly gravitate to what is not true and attach it to what we know is biblically true.

The Intolerant Tolerant

We are not the only ones who need to look at ourselves, our behavior and our views. I've learned something about our secular culture. Those who speak loudest about tolerance are often themselves the most intolerant. Those who say they can't trust by faith in a God they cannot see will place their faith in some of the most amazing teachings that guide their lives. When an unbeliever tells me why he can't believe in God yet he obviously believes in something of his own creation, I tell him he has far more faith than I have; I don't have enough faith to believe what he teaches. There is a myth about faith and non-faith people. In reality, what we really have is faith and faith people. Those who will not place their faith in God place their faith in themselves, their own ideas, even their own view of what amounts to the religion of scientism, or they will place their faith in something else.

The "I don't believe in religion" people are also the ones who say "Don't try to force your religion on me." My reply to them is, "Fair enough. I won't try to force anything on you. But do me a favor; don't try to force your religion on me." The secularist will object, "I don't have a religion." My reply is, "Ask your family, ask your friends, ask those who know you well; they'll tell you what you worship."

Every believing Christians knows that there are people who can point out some inconsistency in our Christian thinking or behavior as a reason for having no interest in our Gospel witness. One elderly woman argued that a hypocrite she met when she was a young girl turned her off from Christianity. We can all find the hypocrites. Avoidance of the Christian faith because of one person's behavior is a weak excuse, and we all know it. No person on this earth is perfect. Hypocrisy is everywhere. It is just that we who follow Jesus shouldn't be like other people. Let the unbelieving secularist be a hypocrite about himself and what he believes; we will follow Jesus.

Some who boast of being the most tolerant are themselves often more intolerant than many whom they condemn as being "intolerant." They not only lie to others about their own intolerance, they lie to themselves. So even though we who are followers of Jesus have to battle through the crowd of other believers who create problems for us and are seen as intolerant, it is not all one-sided. The secular person has his "religion" too, and is intolerant of others, even though he denies it.

If we are shown our weaknesses, and those weaknesses are there, we can also point out the intolerance and the weaknesses in the logic of the secular person who assumes that his own thinking is uncluttered. He too is fooling himself, and we who want to bring Good News to that person don't need to hesitate because we think that secular person has a clear-headed reason for rejecting the Savior. It doesn't take much of a conversation to show clearly that he has a mixed-up philosophy of life. Just because he created that religious mixture himself doesn't make it reasonable or logical. If called to face what he believes about himself, his beliefs will expose their own severe limits and fallacies. He just hasn't bothered to find that out.

Where Are the Prophets

In ancient Israel, the people of YHWH had a tendency to import the gods and idols of other people. God kept sending prophets to call the people back to true worship. Those prophets weren't always appreciated—some were even stoned to death.

Where are today's prophets? Who is calling Christians back to God when they have brought in foreign gods and worship their idols? The ancient Jews kept declaring, "We are God's people." Christians today make that same declaration. But now as then so many still turn to their idols. Back then the idols were made of stone or wood or metal, and they even had their priests. Today we don't make idols of stone or wood or metal, but we do listen to the priests of our age and even quote them.

Yet, even now, God is calling His people back to Himself. Those Christians who have drifted to other gods complain, "Why don't you criticize other people's idols instead of always attacking ours?" The answer is that other people worship their idols because they don't know any better. Followers of the living God do know better. So today's prophets are saying, "Don't look at the gods worshiped by unbelievers, but do look at the foreign gods that are being sought after by believers. Look at the Christian idol's clay feet; look at their weaknesses; look what their media priests are teaching. Don't follow them."

chapter 4

Following the Media Propagandists

I always used to wonder how it was possible that German Christians, living in the land of Luther, taught by such faithful men as Martin Neimoeller and Deitrich Bonhoeffer, could fall for the Nazi propaganda of Joseph Goebbels in the late 1930s and early 1940s. How could they have come to believe the teaching that Jews were vermin who needed to be exterminated? How could they salute and cheer Adolf Hitler and his minions when these men were so obviously evil?

There were two reasons why this happened. Hitler always promoted strong German patriotism and nationalism and Goebbels made certain that the only press, the only radio and the only films that people were exposed to were under the control of his propaganda department. It was illegal to listen to or read anything else. The people were fed the same lies day after day. A lie, told often enough, starts to sound like the truth. Besides, people said, look at all the good that Hitler was doing for the economy and patriotism in the country. Who could fault it?

But I don't wonder about those German Christians anymore. Today I listen to my Christian brothers and sisters quoting untruths in the name of Christianity and Americanism. And over and over again I find that they are listening to only one type of media source, the sources that provide them with the propaganda that they want to hear. They aren't forced to hear only one view, as the Germans were in the days of Hitler; they have chosen to listen to only one view.

Manipulators of the People

There are several kinds of news in our country. News is not the same as propaganda, but sometimes it is very close. In the 1890s, when William Randolph Hearst was trying to build circulation for his newspapers, he needed a war. Not a big war, but some kind of a war. So he sent artist Frederic Remington to Cuba to report on the terrible conditions there. But nothing was happening; there were no atrocities to report.

There is a story—some say it is true, some say it is not—that Remington cabled Hearst to tell him that there was nothing going on and he wanted to come home. Hearst, it is said, famously cabled back, "You furnish the pictures and I'll furnish the war." He got his war, the Spanish-American War.

As patriots and as believers we are exposed to various kinds of news; some of it is true, some of it is not.

Straight News

We know this type of news as a presentation of the basic facts, the "who," "what," "when," "where," "why" and "how" presented in inverted pyramid style. The basics of the story are at the top and more information is given as we read down. Just facts are presented, no opinion.

We don't get a lot of straight news anymore. Television news calls for entertainment so newspapers compete with television by publishing more news features where the basic facts may still be there but they are scattered throughout in a news-feature story. Internet news is basically a headline with more offered if the reader wants it. But even that may be presented more as a feature than as a straight news story.

Interpreted News

Interpreted news occurs when the newspaper or the television network not only tells us what is happening but tells us what it means. So we get information with an interpretation attached to it by the news writer or television presenter.

We all tend to interpret our news, to put it into context. Recently I read an article about a Canadian Member of Parliament. He said, "I have to stop taking my work home with me. My children are picking up my political language." He said that one day he found his five-year-old daughter in tears. Her slightly older brother was standing nearby. The father asked the boy, "Did you hit your sister?" The boy replied, "Well, you have to understand the context."

But putting something into context and interpreting something to mean something else is not the same thing. I was interviewed one time by a well-known Christian magazine. When the article was published I was shocked to see what they had written about me, telling their readers what they said I believed. I called the editor to tell him that they had published false information about me. He replied, "Oh, we know that's not what you said. We thought that's what you meant."

For a full year after that article was published I met people who said, "I read that article about you. I didn't know you believed that." I had to tell them, "I don't believe that." But it is almost impossible to track down everyone who believes something and passes along to others what is not true. Long ago I discovered that a lie can make it halfway around the world before truth can even get its shoes on.

Selected News

We all select our news. Unless we are tweeting about what we had for lunch and the color socks we are wearing that day, most people sort through their information before retelling it. A little boy goes to his first day at school. He colors pictures, learns some numbers, hears a story, and there is a small fire in the teacher's wastepaper basket that she quickly puts out. When he gets home from school and bursts into the kitchen to tell his mother what happened at school that day, guess what he tells her first? That's selected news.

Newspapers and television networks that are governed by a board of directors are usually far more careful about accuracy in what they select and print or show on the television news than a newspaper or television network that is owned by a single individual.

When one person has the final say, as did William Randolph Hearst with his newspapers, we are more likely to get only the news that the owner wants to tell us while he ignores the news he doesn't want to tell.

There is a code called the Society of Professional Journalists Code of Ethics. It's a good code of ethics. I've taught it when I've taught college journalism classes. If a reporter lies or slants the truth or is less than accurate, he can be called out for it. When that happens his editors may fire him. And he probably won't get a job anywhere else.

But not every newspaper or television network signs on to the Journalists Code of Ethics. They don't want to be hindered by having to tell the truth. One network television commentator even denounced the journalism code of ethics on his program. Most of his viewers don't know that he was arguing against a code of ethics that his own network has never subscribed to anyway.

Selected news can easily end up being slanted news. One day, while driving home, I was listening to an interview. Later that night I heard a synopsis of that interview on the television news. I said to Andrea, "That's not what he said. I heard the interview. They have taken it out of context."

I have had the experience of being with a Christian brother who was irate about what he heard on television about something that a political leader said in a speech. I asked him, "Did you hear the speech."

"No."

"Did you pull it up on your computer and read the speech?"

"No."

"Then how do you know what he said?"

"I heard about it from my favorite commentator on the television network that I watch."

I had to say to my Christian brother, "I'm afraid that you've been had. I heard the speech and that isn't what the person said."

But, comes the argument, those were his words—yes, they were his words, sort of, if you select words out of context and then cut and paste them together. I've heard it done, and some of the cutting and pasting is really very clever.

Remember the old cutting and pasting joke about Judas? It goes, "Judas hanged himself; go thou and do likewise, and what thou doest, do quickly."

Now, if I were not interested in accuracy or fairness or context I would say, "What's your problem? Those words are in the Bible aren't they?"

"Yes."

"Well, then, I am quoting Scripture."

"Yes. You are quoting Scripture, but you are not quoting it accurately and you are taking it out of context."

Would a Christian do that? Would a believer who is seeking to follow Jesus take someone's words out of context, cut them apart and then paste those words back together again in a new way while arguing that those words were spoken by that person? And would a Christian patriot do that in order to skewer the politician he doesn't like, attacking him for what he said when, in fact, he didn't say that at all?

Directed News

This happens when a newspaper owner or someone who owns a television network decides what he wants the news to be and then directs his people to present it that way. If he can't find substantiation, he creates it.

It is not easy to comment on Fox News since so many Christians make that network their primary news source and then quote to others what they hear on Fox. But as a journalist and a fellow believer, I have to expose the problem. Painful as it is, the reality points to managed and directed news on Fox. Here is an example of that network's reporting that was directed and arranged and, of necessity, exposed by the *Chicago Tribune*. During a football game, Jay Cutler, quarterback for the Chicago Bears, was injured and had to leave the game. That seemed like a straightforward news story. Except that either Fox News owner Rupert Murdoch, or those who serve him, did not want the story to be that of an injury. To their way of thinking Cutler was afraid to stay in the game. He was a coward. But how could they report such a story when it wasn't true?

They did it by attributing the story of Cutler's lack of courage to other media, particularly the Chicago-area newspapers, including the *Chicago Tribune*. They held up sports pages with a headline about Cutler's fear of getting back into the game. The announcer said, "These are the actual headlines from the local papers in Chicago." Only it wasn't true. Those newspapers never published such a story.

The *Chicago Tribune* went after Fox News demanding to know where they got the story they were quoting. Where did that headline they were pointing to come from? Finally, the Fox News people admitted that they had fabricated those newspaper pages themselves. Except for the *Chicago Tribune* revealing what was done, Fox viewers would have had no way of knowing that the announcer's false newspaper attribution was untrue.

Or, here is another example of managing the news. When the second-term election took place during Barack Obama's presidency all of the polls showed the president winning with an electoral-college count of as much as 332 votes, whereas none of the polls showed his opponent, Mitt Romney, with any more than 206 votes, except in the Murdoch media. Even though their own Fox polls showed Obama up by large numbers, they didn't report those numbers. Their own stories showed Romney ahead. Some of their reports put Romney up over Obama by as much as a double-digit lead. As a result, their politicians and pundits, their own news people and their viewers were absolutely shocked at the outcome of the election. The final count mirrored all the polls exactly. Yet because the Murdoch media people offered only their own opinions, not even their own polls, and their followers believed those opinions, there was great consternation among their viewers the day after the election.

Because many of the Fox news followers are Christians, and they repeat what they hear on the news programs, there is a need to go online, research and check what is heard. People who don't follow Fox and do check to get as broad a view of the news as they can often marvel at what they refer to as the "gullible Christians." They carry that view about Christians with them into any discussions that we might have with them about the Savior.

When My Doubts Began to Grow

I first became suspicious about this managed news some years ago while walking on a treadmill at the neighborhood health club. Somebody had Fox News on the television. I don't remember the issue being discussed but I did become aware that all of the views being expressed were from Republican government officials. I wondered, "Why don't they balance that with a Democrat or two." No sooner had that thought crossed my mind when the presenter said, "And now, to tell us what the view of the Democratic Party is on this issue…" I thought, "Oh, good. They are going to balance their report." But I was wrong. The speaker continued "… here is Republican senator so-and-so to tell us what the Democrats are saying about this." I threw up my hands in disgust.

A parody news site called "National Report," knowing full well that Fox News would report anything negative about President Obama, created a spoof and sent it to Fox. It stated that because of the October 2013 government shutdown, a museum of Muslim culture was closed. So President Obama funded it out of his own pocket to keep it open. Fox bit, didn't check to verify, and reporter Anna Kooiman reported that story on the air. When Fox realized that they'd been spoofed, Kooiman corrected herself via Twitter. But those who heard the report probably continued to spread the false news because it fit what they already wanted to believe.

Even though many of my fellow believers will disagree with me, I've determined that I cannot be a follower of Rupert Murdoch who owns News Corps and its many subsidiaries including Fox television and, in recent years, the *Wall Street Journal* (WSJ). I did purposely subscribe to the WSJ to see if I was wrong about the coverage given to events since Murdoch took over. Not only was the news selected and presented more as opinion pieces, the editorial content was the guided content that he expected his people to say. As I check what he puts in the newspapers he owns and the television news that he rules, I too often find half-truths or total fabrications that can be easily checked out through any number of online sources.

But many Christians don't check. They prefer to believe that they alone are getting unbiased, fair and accurate reporting—because that's what Murdoch's reporters tell them they are getting. Friends tell me, "We only watch Fox News. Do you watch Fox?" I can only reply, "Not usually." But what I really want to say is, "I'm not a follower of Rupert Murdoch; I'm a follower of Jesus."

For the faithful followers of Rupert Murdoch, it doesn't matter that Fox News and the *Wall Street Journal* follow the same rules as those imposed on the *Times* of London or BSkyB television news in the U.K. Never mind the scandals that have exposed the illegal behavior of the people who worked for Murdoch's news outlets in the U.K., including illegal phone hacking. When the scandal over *News of the World* was brought to light, Murdoch shut the paper down. But the lead executive of that newspaper, along with seven others, was soon put on trial for conspiracy.

The phone hacking not only included celebrities but included hacking the telephone of a murdered schoolgirl. Ethics and morality are not held in high esteem in the world of media that some Christians believe are the only true purveyors of truth. When secularists mock Murdoch with the exclamation "Rupert strikes again," because of the latest directed news in his media, the Christians accept what they are given almost as holy writ. We have lost our credibility with the very people who need our Gospel message.

When Rupert Murdoch bought the *Wall Street Journal*, he made some sweeping changes in the content of the newspaper and the staff that for years had been producing a quality newspaper. In her book, *War at the Wall Street Journal*, Sarah Ellison, a ten-year veteran of the paper, writes of the pressure put on the staff who were eventually weeded out to be replaced by those who would follow the wishes of the new owner, Rupert Murdoch.

In the book she tells us that the order was for the WSJ editors to follow the same rule as Fox News. It was the ruling that if there was anything negative about Republicans, it would not be reported. If there was anything positive about Democrats, it would not be reported. It was explained that Robert Thompson, whom Murdoch brought in from the *Times* of London, objected to any story that was anti-Republican. Even if a report had too many quotations from Democrats it, would be cut.

According to Ellison, Marcus Baruchli, who spent most of his career at the *Wall Street Journal,* "...admitted that Murdoch was coloring every move." It was explained that nobody believed a Murdoch editor had "a thought or utterance that didn't originate from Murdoch."

When my friends tell me all the good news about Republicans and all the bad news about Democrats, I know what they have been watching and reading. And, since each medium will quote the other, with WSJ quoting Fox and Fox quoting WSJ, readers and viewers think that what they are being told is accurate since it is backed up by the other source. Christians don't seem to realize that whether they are reading WSJ or watching Fox News they are getting the same information that is dictated by Rupert Murdoch.

Followers of Made-up News

During the government shutdown in October 2013, the *Wall Street Journal* came up with a quote from a "senior government official" who declared, "We are winning," and "it doesn't matter how long the shutdown lasts." The White House quickly denied such a statement, but that didn't stop speaker John Boehner from holding up the WSJ and using it to bludgeon the White House and to gain points with those who wanted to believe that such a statement was made. Did anyone name the official? Did anyone pay attention to the White House denial? Did speaker Boehner really not know how the *Wall Street Journal* works?

Maybe he didn't know. I remember reading a story in the *Times* of London. It was a story stating that a European government was supporting the terrorist group al Qaeda. That government complained, stating that the story wasn't true. There was no substantiation to the story, nothing to back it up. It was simply a hit-and-run story that planted the charge and then left it. I wondered how this could be. This wasn't the *Times* that I knew. They always had well-substantiated writing. Then it hit me. Could it be? I checked and, sure enough, the *Times* had been bought by Rupert Murdoch. That explained the problem to me, but probably not to other readers.

Those stories can be multiplied. So many professing Christians follow the purveyors of made-up news and refuse to check any other sources. As a result they often tend to be out of the loop insofar as having a true understanding of what is happening around them. And because many Christians are very vocal about what they believe to be true, and because many of their secular hearers have taken the time to check and find out what is true and what is not, the Christians are written off as a people who live in their own world, unconnected to reality.

Worse, by having so much inaccurate media clutter as a part of our Christian speech, we who are followers of Jesus, who want to obey the Great Commission to go into all the world and preach the Gospel, are not heard—not because our Gospel isn't true but because we have added to it false beliefs that the people we are speaking to know are not true. It is very difficult to explain that, "Even though much of what we keep telling you about politics and culture is not true, what we are telling you about Jesus is true." We may think that people are rejecting our Savior, but many are rejecting all the other information that we have wrapped around the Savior so they cannot clearly see Him.

I won't spend my time watching television to find out what Rupert Murdoch's people tell me is right or wrong. I will check the sources myself and find out what is true and what is not. In these days when we can so easily check facts, that is not a hard thing to do. Also, as a believer, I will not keep quoting falsehoods that I find because they suit my preconceived ideas of what I want to be true about our culture, our politics and our world.

Questioning the President's Birth

Much ink has been spent on various attempts to prove that President Obama is not an American citizen and therefore is not eligible to be the president of the United States. Where no evidence could be found that disproved his Hawaiian birth certificate, the general consensus among many Christians was that there must be evidence somewhere, it just hasn't been found yet. His mother was American, his father Kenyan, and therefore the president must not be a true-born American citizen.

But when the junior senator from Texas, Ted Cruz, made a name for himself with his 21-hour filibuster against Obamacare, some Christians thought he might be a fine presidential candidate. Yet none whom I've met have bothered to check his background or the legitimacy about his place of birth. His father was born in Cuba, even fighting for Castro as a youth. His mother was born in Delaware. But Ted Cruz was born in Calgary, Alberta, Canada. Cruz's father became a U.S. citizen in 2005. So is Ted Cruz eligible to be president? No one seems to be asking. The same people, who won't let go of the issue concerning Barack Obama won't even raise the same question about Ted Cruz. The secular people who listen to Christians on this issue smile at the gymnastics vocal Christians go through in their attempt to prove one person an alien, the other an American, when, at least, Obama was born on U.S. territory.

Unfortunately, secular people can see what we are doing with our thought processes. When George Orwell wrote his book *1984*, the year was 1949. He was projecting to a future time. Orwell used the term "Doublethink," which means, "...to tell deliberate lies while genuinely believing in them, to forget any fact that is inconvenient." Honest people don't knowingly practice "doublethink." And Christians ought to be honest people.

Rejecting What We Don't Want to Believe

To be fair, there are secular media capturing the minds of people who can be just as vocal as Christians about what is true and what is not. I recently saw a bumper sticker that read, "I don't trust the liberal, leftist media." Well, I don't trust all the media either. There is plenty of biased news reporting to go around. But I have found that I can usually get secular people to do the research, to find out what is accurate and what is not, and to readjust their thinking based on balanced examination. We can all do that by keying in words or statements on our computers and reading the background that is available on the matter. Too often, however, asking Christians to do that with the media they watch or read is like hitting a stone wall. They already believe that they are right, they don't need to check, and so they damage their biblical witness when they declare that their political or social information is right and true. If we are going to be people like that, how can anyone believe what we are saying about Jesus?

For example, when so much was being leveled at then Secretary of State Hillary Clinton about the embassy attack in Benghazi, Libya, those criticisms were led by Representative Jason Chaffetz of Utah. The questions were, what did she know and when did she know it? That's fair enough, except that his attacks on her also offered Chaffetz a smokescreen. Why weren't there military on hand to protect the embassy? That's a given for embassy protection. It was Chaffetz who, in a cavalier manner, said that such staffing was too expensive. He said, "Look, we have to make priorities and choices in this country." So, in 2012, he and his colleagues in the House of Representatives cut 331 million dollars from the budget that funded embassy protection, after cutting 128 million the year before. When reminded that the embassy in Benghazi was asking for more security before it was attacked, he went on Fox News to blame others, including the White House and the State Department, for what happened at the embassy.

Now, in attack mode, instead of looking at the protection of the embassy and the funding cuts that made it a prime target for terrorists, questions were being asked about who said what, and when. Emails were released on the talking points, including the handwritten edits of those emails. But when Chaffetz and his colleagues produced those emails on the evening news, they were different. Apparently, according to a comparison made in a CBS news report and comments by White House press secretary Jay Carney, the accusers of Mrs. Clinton showed copies of the emails that they had further edited or altered themselves. Chaffetz and his colleagues made the public think that the emails were part of a conspiracy to hide what was known while all the time the emails they were using to make their point were emails that they had created or edited themselves. All this was happening while also covering up the cuts in support of military strength that would have helped the embassy protect itself in the first place. We can't be responsible for what politicians do. But as Christians we are responsible not to be carriers of misinformation if we can instead do diligent research before speaking.

Practice Makes Perfect

It is a proven tactic that the best defense is a strong offense, and the people who cut the embassy protection funds kept the pressure elsewhere in order to keep the spotlight off what they had done themselves that made the embassy vulnerable to attack.

This sort of cover up and attack had been quite perfected from experience gained during the 9/11 tragic events. There was a call for an independent investigation—who knew what, was there any information being withheld—because enough leaks were coming out to imply that some knew more than they let on. House Majority Leader Tom DeLay, representative from Texas, tried to malign the investigating commission with accusations of partisanship, saying that the "politicization of the commission undermines the war effort [in Iraq] and endangers our troops." A commission was appointed, but it was weak and was controlled and underfunded by the White House. Then, to make sure nothing pointed toward any Republican, David Horowitz, author of *How to Beat the Democrats and Other Subversive Ideas,* wrote in FrontPageMagazine.com that the Democrats were the "...significant players in the debacle of 9/11. And no one is more singularly responsible for America's vulnerability on that fateful day than the Democratic president Bill Clinton, and his White House staff."

So the people who wanted an investigation blocked or delayed went on the attack of the previous administration as the cause of 9/11. Unfortunately, this isn't as humorous as it might seem because too many Christians believe what they are told by the media that promotes this kind of propaganda. We have a choice not to accept it, but too many of us do anyway.

The horror of 9/11 stands out in my mind particularly because Andrea and I were on a plane in Copenhagen, Denmark, that had just pushed back from the gate when the captain came on the speaker and told us that America was under attack and we were not allowed to fly. So all flights to the U.S were cancelled, clear skies were ordered over the nation, and we stayed in Copenhagen for four days wondering what was happening at home and waiting for flights to be resumed over U.S. territory.

Imagine our feelings when later we heard that when no flights were allowed anywhere in U.S. skies, Osama bin Laden's family representatives were sitting at an investors conference at the Ritz Carlton Hotel in Washington DC. They were immediately allowed to fly back to Jeddah before they could be questioned by the FBI. Not true, said the FBI in later reports. There were more than 160 Saudis in the U.S. at the time of the attack and, although some were escorted to airports "for their safety," none left before the skies were declared open on September 13 and they were able to arrange charters. Checking does clarify lots of things even when clarification corrects an urban legend but doesn't help with attitudes about what happened.

Closed Minded Is Not a Virtue

Simply accepting what we read, hear or see without checking just because we assume the people who are telling us what to believe seem to be ethical people, even fellow believers, can lead us into a lot of misinformation. When we pass along that information, we are contributors to false teaching.

There are many examples where Christians have gotten on board with something only to discover later, after others already knew, that they were wrong.

Based on his book *The Roots of Obama's Rage,* Dinesh D'Souza created his movie "2016: Obama's America" made up of selected and pasted-together material and speculation that he put into his film without regard to context. When D'Souza was later caught in other lies, especially with a woman in his hotel room who was not his wife, and was dismissed by the Christian college where he was president, he lost some of his credence to most believers who at first wanted to believe that what his "documentary" about

President Obama showed was accurate. His documentary is an example of selected or created news.

I found the same kind of selection in a Christian college newsletter that was sent to me bearing all the usual and now well-worn diatribes against President Obama. What the piece didn't say was that a recent president of that college was invited to "retire" because for 19 years he had been carrying on an affair with his son's wife until she committed suicide. Yet this college is referred to as "A bedrock of conservatism and family values." Apparently that form of immorality was not deemed important when that college newsletter listed all that it perceived was wrong with America, especially under the presidency of Barack Obama.

When Minnesota Representative Michelle Bachmann criticized government spending and told the Minneapolis *Star-Tribune* that neither she nor her family took "one penny" of handouts, she forgot to mention the $260,000 in government subsidies claimed by her family farm. Nor did she mention the $30,000 her counselor husband received from the state of Minnesota. Since the average food stamp program in America has been about $133 per person per month, the farm-subsidy handout that Michelle Bachmann received from the government would have fed many poor families. Yet she spoke against a farm bill that "exemplifies the very worst of Washington ways," and her Tea Party colleagues wanted to cut back the food stamp program. Most Christians never bothered to check this out. Christians, who should care about the poor as Jesus did seem to hear only about the "expense" of food stamps.

When Michelle Bachmann decided not to run for Congress again, many evangelical Christians were troubled. She stood up for family values, the Christians insisted. But those family values didn't seem to embrace the poor trying to support their families on low wages. And if any applied for food stamps or any other government help, they were criticized and such programs were targeted to be blocked. Is it a Christian family value to say, "I get my large government handouts but I'm going to make sure that you don't receive any small ones"?

Because I lived for 33 years in Minnesota, I pay extra attention to what is said by Minnesota political leaders. Bachmann has been the butt of many jokes by unbelievers and is often an embarrassment to believers. Using her platform to say any outrageous thing that comes to mind may be dismissed by fellow Christians but is more fodder for the secular person who makes her out to be one of our "Christian leaders." When she went on radio to announce that we are living in the end times, she made her point to prove that these are the end times by stating, "President Obama waived a ban on arming terrorists in order to allow weapons to go to the Syrian opposition. Your listeners, U.S. taxpayers, are now paying to give arms to terrorists, including al Qaeda." Many Christians believed what she said because she is "one of us."

Even Brian Tashman, who is known as a right-wing spokesperson, said that Bachmann "…was stretching the truth in her accusations against Obama." He explained that the aid was going only to vetted rebels not affiliated with terrorist organizations and that it was "non-lethal, defensive and protective aid." Christians may know that Bachmann is creating her own truth, but many will accept it anyway. The secular person sees it as one more proof that Christians will believe anything, no matter how false, and can't be depended on to speak truthfully. Certainly the unbeliever will not be able to tell when we are repeating false information and when we are presenting arguments that are biblical and true.

The same is true for values. At the three-day Value Voters 2013 Summit the purpose was to see how Christian values should or could influence government, which is fair enough. But they didn't cover such issues as the poor or any other issues that we find in Scripture. The members of the religious right who were in attendance were taking the political points of the Tea Party and applying Christian principles to them. In other words, they didn't seem to be trying to formulate policy based on Christian values; rather, they first accepted the policies and then tried to find ways to apply Christian values to them. It wasn't moral values from the top down; it was from the bottom up, an attempt to baptize what already was being implemented. When the secular people see this and look at the teachings of Jesus, they don't understand Christianity. But that's because they haven't encountered Christianity. They have encountered only established political positions that the religious people try to make "Christian" by the jargon they apply to it. The world rejects our jargon. But that's entirely different from rejecting our Christ.

Selected News about Military Spending

If a U.S. senator steps onto the Senate floor to speak out against all of the wasteful government spending on military equipment that the military doesn't even want, he is likely to be attacked for "weakening our military." When Bill Hemmer on Fox showed a chart of military spending, he declared that the U.S. was lagging behind China and Russia. What he neglected to tell his viewers was that U.S. military spending is greater than the next 12 top-spending countries in the world combined. Christians who boast that "We only watch Fox news" don't realize how willing they are to be taken in. But their secular neighbors surely know.

What is not said about military spending is that many of the military contracts that are kept in place are going to districts of the very congressional people who decry the "wasteful spending." They, in fact, want that "wasteful spending" because for those congressional people, when millions of dollars in contracts for materiel not wanted by the military go to their own districts, the companies that are awarded those contracts are smart enough to send large donations back to their benefactors' reelection coffers.

When unbelievers reject what they perceive as our Christian willingness to accept what we are told, and blame us for blindly believing what we haven't bothered to examine, we assume that they must be rejecting our Christian faith. But most don't even think about Jesus; instead, they are thinking about us.

Not realizing why people in our culture think of us as they do is not in keeping with the call every Christian has from Jesus to go and preach the Gospel. If we don't know what is happening around us and refuse to be wise about what we embrace and continue to quote information that is either untrue or cloudy, we lose our witness. Why should anyone want to hear our biblical truth when we are already known as people who are willing to quote what is shady or outright false?

Unequipped Missionaries in Our Own Land

We know the dangers of sending out unequipped missionaries who don't know the language or the customs of the culture where they go. We can see what happens if someone goes to another place ignorant of that place and the people, including how they live and think. The person who only wants to tell others about Jesus but doesn't equip himself with what the culture of a certain society believes and practices makes himself look foolish and often causes great harm to others—especially to others who do know what they are doing when they go out with the Gospel.

While teaching in a Central-Asian country, I learned that the Orthodox Church and the Muslim clerics there issued a joint newspaper report that showed how both were trying to keep radicals out of their country. The Muslims didn't want fanatics, those Islamists who would inflame their Muslim communities. The Orthodox leadership didn't want most evangelical missionaries because they were disruptive, didn't understand the people and didn't seem to even want to understand. They just came with their own packaged ways and message. The local Christian missionary I was with in that country, who is having a very effective work, said the Orthodox Church was right. Too many evangelicals attempted to come in with no understanding of the culture or even a desire to understand the people. For this evangelical missionary whom I was with and who did know the people, the cultural ways and the language, other evangelicals who came crashing in unprepared caused him a lot of trouble and hindered his work.

It is the same in our own country and culture. American evangelicals who think they know what is happening around them because they listen only to selected information cause a lot of trouble for other Christians who sincerely want to announce the Good News of Jesus. The Christians who are willing to learn the culture and the language of their neighbors are the ones who will stop adding to the Gospel with their social and political falsehoods, stop attacking the people in the culture who aren't behaving as Christians want them to behave and start being what Jesus called us to be—His disciples. We need to be missionaries in our own land and understand the language, the culture and how to love the people we want to reach.

The Books We Read

When I was serving as a judge of nonfiction books for the ECPA Christian Book Award program, formerly known as the Gold Medallion Awards, I found some strong, well-thought-through works. But I also saw some absolute fluff written mostly by

Christian media personalities who have a broad following and thus could ensure publishers that they could sell a lot of books. I found much shallow thinking, even silliness, in some of their books. Yet those are the books that are getting sold because marketing is the tail that wags the dog in Christian publishing today and a quality book by an author who does not have a big platform will either not be published in the first place or, if published, will not be given much help in the way of marketing beyond what the author can provide himself. The empty books, written by some of those who do have big platforms, will be published and promoted. Since so many Christian book publishers are now owned by secular houses where management doesn't care about content, only about sales and profits, the empty Christian books are kept in stock because big sales can be promised by the author. Anyone of intelligence reading many of these books could easily come to believe that Christians are an empty-headed people.

When my own early books were accepted for publication, it was by the editorial side of the publishing house. Then the marketing side saw to it that the book was promoted. That has now entirely changed. Today the editorial staff at most publishing houses only edits and prints the books that marketing approves. The writer is asked what television and radio he can get on, what speaking engagements he has, who he knows who can help promote the book and how many sales he can expect to generate through his own social media such as Facebook and Twitter. An agent will ask the same questions since he is basically a first-filter for the publishing house and he knows that without a sales-based potential a publisher will not even look at a book.

Some of the smaller publishing houses will still work with a lesser-known author, but it is difficult to get those books into the bookstores, even Christian bookstores, because profit is the critical driving force. One of the changes now coming on strong is subsidy publishing where the writer pays all of the up-front costs to produce the book. At one time it was known as "vanity press" because it appealed to a writer to have a book in print even though the book had been rejected by standard publishers.

Today there are still printers who will print a book for a writer without so much as an edit. Then the writer has a book that causes him to be embarrassed when friends point out the poor writing and editing. But there are also some subsidy houses that will provide quality editors, attractive graphics for covers, the ISBN number and all that a standard publisher provides. It just costs the author quite a large sum up front. If the writer feels that his books are going to sell well, then the up-front costs don't matter. If the book doesn't sell, then the author has a garage full of books with no way to market them.

Enter e-publishing. Because today we are basically making one electronic copy, whether that copy is going from computer to press for a printed book or remains electronic for an e-reader, it is a different day for publishing. The self-publishing author can create one electronic copy and let a program such as offered by Amazon.com print a copy as a buyer purchases the book or, if he prefers, to download it on to his electronic reader. There is no storage or inventory.

More and more authors, even many who once only published with standard publishers, are going that e-publishing route because they have more control over their book (not having to bow to the wishes of a standard publisher who wants changes made to the book that a writer might not want to make), the cover the author prefers, and can even update the book easily because it is only one electronic copy. Returns for many who go with e-publishing have proven more profitable as well since there is less holdback than is taken by the print publishers. And, since marketing is mostly up to the author these days anyway (easy for the TV personality to do, not so easy for the writer who does not have such a platform), the writer figures that since he is doing all or most of the marketing, he should not have to let a standard publisher keep most of the royalties.

I remember one of my books going quickly into a second printing. That was rather exciting until I got my first royalty statement from that particular publishing house. They claimed that no copies of my book had sold. But, I wondered, how could that be if they went into a second printing? In comparing notes with another author who published a book with that same company, I found that she experienced the exact same thing. There is no recourse; I had no way of knowing whether or not books had sold. I could only point to books I purchased at discount to have available at writers' conferences or other speaking venues. Since no royalties are given for the author's discounted purchases anyway, there is no way to prove that the company sold books but didn't pay the author's royalties. All I knew was that for a company that claimed to have not sold any books, they certainly went quickly into a second printing. That was an example of a Christian book house that had sold out to a large secular publisher. My book's imprint was the Christian house, but the royalties were paid or not paid by the larger secular house.

Fortunately, God is opening these new doors for writers where they can publish and market their books electronically if they choose to and bypass the standard publishers and bookstores. There are some serious thinking Christians who are writing, and their books need to be read. I found some of them while judging the Award books. If Christians will read selectively, they will find quality that will cause their thinking to expand and be challenged. They may have to look beyond the regular bookstores to the electronic stores to find those quality books, but they can be found.

Magazines and Their Future

As with newspapers, fewer print magazines are being published today than in the past. Some are going out of business entirely or going to e-zines, which are electronic magazines. I enjoy writing for magazines and have done so for many years. But many of the once-popular Christian magazines are no longer in print.

There have always been Christian publications that did not pay their authors. They haven't had enough funds to do it. They would always tell an author that they didn't pay and the author knew that the articles he submitted to those publications would earn no payment. That was always acceptable to me because the magazines stated their nonpaying position up front and I could submit an article to them or not, being fully aware that I would not be paid.

But now I am facing a problem that I never faced in the past. There are a few magazines that tell their authors they do pay for articles, but then they don't pay. Not all have contracts with writers so the relationship is based on trust. I have contacted editors who simply ignored my request for their promised payment or who have told me that they don't pay for articles. "But," I reply, "You advertised to authors that you do pay." The response I've gotten is that the payment statement I saw was a mistake. Many believers are blessed by what is in Christian publications. The article writers have done careful work. But those same readers may not know that a few Christian magazines are neither honest nor fair with the authors who supply them with good work. One of those I've dealt with recently has already ceased publication.

Our Entertainment World

There are a number of solid believers in the entertainment world. I have heard Christian film writers asked, "How can you allow some of the filth that is on the movie screens?" One Christian writer being challenged smiled and said, "You should see what we have been able to keep out."

Studies show that often the family-type films gross more than films that portray a sordid side of life. Many families are not going to the movie theatres as much, but teens, including Christian teens, are. An understanding of what corrupts the mind is not something that always influences the selections many Christians make about what they see at the movie theaters or on their own television screens.

Hollywood has become a propaganda machine for open sex, destruction of life and the blasphemy of God. I expect it, but I don't like it. When people said there was civility in language and behavior years ago, that can't be disputed. When even on the streets we pick up all the filth peddled by films and television, we sometimes can't tell the difference between a church attender and a God hater. The entertainment industry has influenced—some would say brainwashed—people, both Christian and non-Christian.

There is a lot of evil in our world. The decline into depravity is all around us. No one can deny that. As believers we certainly have to be burdened by it. To add to our burden is the number of professing Christians who lack discernment and are no different in their entertainment selections than those in the secular culture. We are a called-out people but we have not always demonstrated what that means. Too often we are a pleasure-seeking people who want to be entertained by both the world and even by our churches. I remember one mega-church pastor telling a group of ministers how his Sunday morning worship service attendance will rise and fall each week depending on the sermon topic.

Just as pleasure is about "me," we have somehow changed the meaning of worship from the adoration and praise of God to what entertains and pleases us. Churches that tumble all over themselves to add more entertainment for the pleasure-seeking crowd will always be behind when it comes to discipling believers. We can never out-world the world, nor should we be trying. It is the biblical depth, the mystery, the holiness of God that is the contrast people crave deep down inside. When they enter the movie theater, the rock concert or the church built on entertainment, they don't have what deep down inside they long to find.

God's Name Is Not an Empty Word

One day, while eating in a restaurant with friends, we were having a good visit when from the next table came a loud exclamation using the name of God. We all turned because the whole restaurant was polluted by that person who was using God's name. So, loudly enough for the people at the offender's table to hear, I said, "She's praying." To that, one of the friends at our table replied just as loudly, "Well does she have to pray in such a loud voice." I wonder if those in the restaurant got the message.

But most often the person using God's name in that way doesn't even know she is calling on God. She doesn't even know who God is. She will have learned from films and television, and then from the culture that feeds on films and television, that God is neither sacred nor is His name holy. He is just another swear word.

We who know who God is may not use His name as a swear word (although I have heard professing Christians do it), but do we present God's example, God's teachings or God's revelation of Himself as something less than holy or sacred? Our speech reveals what is inside. What we repeat shows what we think.

Following the Media

When the 50th Anniversary of the March on Washington took place, past presidents Jimmy Carter and Bill Clinton spoke; so did President Obama. That sparked Bill O'Reilly to tell his Fox viewers that no Republican or conservative had been invited. And, since he is like an oracle from God to many Christians, they believed him.

But O'Reilly didn't speak the truth. Both Presidents George H. W. Bush and George W. Bush were invited to speak that day; they declined. John Boehner, Speaker of the House, was invited. He declined. Eric Cantor, House Majority Leader, was invited, but he too declined, meeting instead with gas and oil lobbyists who over the years have given $600,000 to his campaigns. Senator John McCain and former Florida governor Jeb Bush were invited, but they too declined. In fact, every member of Congress was invited.

Does the truth get in the way of O'Reilly when he says such things to his viewers? Apparently truth doesn't matter to those who listen to him either. When he declared that no Republicans or conservatives had been invited to that historic event, most of his listeners would probably have believed him without checking to see if what he told them was true. Later he did find out the truth and admitted that he "simply assumed" that Republicans were excluded.

Am I the kind of media follower who feeds on the false teachings of some of the news presenters or columnists or editorial people? Or am I a person with a different mind, a mind not captured by the propagandists? Am I one who wants to live by the apostle's urging, "Do not conform any longer to the pattern of this world, but be transformed by the renewing of your mind. Then you will be able to test and approve what God's will is—his good, pleasing and perfect will" (Rom. 12:2).

Will I ever be able to test and approve what God's will is if I am filling my mind with what is false?

Evangelical Writers and Israel

I remember the first invitation I received to visit Israel. I went with a group of fellow journalists. Israel's ministry of tourism offered the trip and it was very special. We lived well, traveled well, ate well and met with government officials. The only request made to us was that we write about Israel. I was happy to do it. This happened three times, and as much as I enjoyed the experience, I began to realize that I was not being an honest writer. What we were expected to write was always positive, never a balance. I could not do it anymore.

But I've watched a few other evangelicals continue to enjoy the perks of such travel and continue to write positive even flattering articles about Israel. Soon it became clear to me, based on their writings, that these fellow Christians were making the current citizens of Israel into the same people as those who followed Moses out of Egypt and then Joshua into the Promised Land. Historically, even though often rebellious and needing a call from the prophets to return to God, those early people of Israel were a theocracy. God was the head and the Jews were His people.

I began to realize that modern Israel is not a theocracy. God is not the head of most Israeli citizens. Indeed, they are mostly a secular people, not a religious one. I also began to realize that those evangelicals who enjoy the perks of travel at Israel's expense are writing articles, books and newsletters making Israel into what even the people of Israel themselves do not claim to be.

In *The Economist,* November 16, 2013, I read that many Jews in the U.S. do not approve of some of the actions of the government of Israel, including some of the building in the West Bank. This was based on a Pew poll of Jewish-American voters. Then the article stated, "On many measures, white evangelical Protestants are a more reliably pro-Israel voter block (possibly because white evangelicals are twice as likely as American Jews to believe that God gave Israel to the Jews.)" So it is not that

American Jews are trying to make Israel into a biblical theocracy. It is the evangelicals who are trying to do that. (The numbers reported in the December 2013 issue of *Christianity Today* shows that 40 percent of American Jews believe that "Israel was given to the Jewish people by God." But 82 percent of white evangelicals believe this.)

In the U.S., evangelical money and support flow to writers and speakers who can show photos of themselves with government officials and can communicate that they have an inside track with Israeli leadership. Yet all the time they are really just repeating what they are given to say about the people and the land.

I am seeing also that there are Arab Christians, and other peoples as well, who are suffering in Israel, yet I can understand that Israel is an important buffer in an Islamic region and a friend of the U.S. Still, Israel is not what so many evangelicals are making it out to be. In fact, I can no longer tell how much the evangelical spokespersons believe about the role of today's Israel in God's plan and how much they are simply enjoying all the good food, expensive hotels and free travel lavished upon them by the tourism ministry of Israel in return for telling the story that Israel wants them to tell. And, of course, there are the profits at home they receive through the donations sent to them as "spokespersons for Israel."

Am I a biblical Christian if I make a people into a theocracy when they themselves are mostly secular? Am I an honest writer if I repeat information for a price? Am I even a patriot of the United States if, as some have done, I criticize my own country for not always doing what Israel wants my country to do on their behalf?

And what about a clear witness to the saving work of the Messiah? Do politics and rich perks replace the call from Jesus to proclaim the redeeming truth beginning in Jerusalem and then Judea and then to the ends of the earth? Will I be the kind of American who stands against my country, stands instead for Israel, and do it for what amounts to bribery? Can I forget my calling to be prophetic and evangelistic to the Jewish people whom God dearly loves? Will I someday tell God that I liked the free meals, the expensive hotels and the heady atmosphere of meeting with government leaders more than I wanted to be honest, balanced and a clear presenter of "thus saith the Lord"?

We need to be balanced and biblical writers, but not all Christians want to do that. Jesus died for all, but for some evangelicals, the nation of Israel is seen as good enough as long as the tourism people keep sending invitations to visit at their expense. The world sees what we do and realizes more than some evangelicals do that our Gospel is often selective, depending on who is offering the nice perks.

Behavior Follows What Is within Us

We who are "in Christ" are not to become like the world; we are not to act as though we do not belong to the One who came so that "...they may have life, and have it to the full" (John 10:10). We have God and His word to guide us. We are a different people in a world that is often all the same.

Media propaganda can't be avoided. But what they peddle doesn't have to be swallowed without thought either. What they teach doesn't become the guideline for the life of the Christian who has a transformed mind. We are a royal priesthood, a chosen generation. Why? Is it so that we can then surrender what we are and follow the propagandists who lead us not toward a deeper walk with God but away from it?

What we see, hear and read from the directed-news media may capture others, but that propaganda won't capture the one whose heart is already captured by the word of God. Will we be people of the truth or people captured by falsehoods? We cannot be both. The apostle John explained, "Whoever claims to live in him must live as Jesus did" (1 John 2:6).

Being faithful Christians means we ought also to be honest patriots. We should love our country, our flag, and understand who we are and what makes us a special people. That means we ought to know our history and the role of God in our history. We don't make up a history that isn't true or live in denial about a history that is true. If we do, we will most likely miss seeing the great workings of God in our nation's history.

chapter 5

Forgetting Our History
(Christian and American)

Where in the Bible do we read that America is the new Israel? Where do we read that Americans are God's chosen people? I have to ask because I am often given the impression that 2 Chronicles 7:14 refers to the United States. There we read, "If my people, who are called by my name, will humble themselves and pray and seek my face and turn from their wicked ways, then I will hear from heaven, and I will forgive their sin and will heal their land." This passage of Scripture points to those whom God calls "My people."

The healing of any land begins with the healing of God's people. It is God's people in that land who need revival and renewal. For a nation to be revived, her people must first be revived. It isn't the secular people who need to be renewed; it is the people who are called by God's name. There has to first be life before that life can be revived. Some Christians would prefer to look at the nation rather than look at themselves. But it is those who name the Name and are called "My people" who need to be revived if we are to become a nation of forgiven people.

American Christians tend to think of the nation as godly, especially that it started out that way. It didn't. It had God's people in it, but not all who were in it were God's people. Nostalgia about our land, especially when it is not based on reality, can actually keep us from humbling ourselves, seeking His face and turning from our wicked ways.

The founders of our nation spoke of Providence. They spoke of Deity. But did they speak of Jesus, the Messiah? Or did they call Him "Savior"? At what point do we praise our Founding Fathers as men of religion and at what point do we start calling them Christians? Because if we do that, wanting them to be more Christian than they actually were, we will be known as people who don't know our history very well. A person who makes up history as he wants it to be, not as it was, will not have a strong voice when speaking of the need for a Christian America. In fact, he may be holding us back from experiencing the hand of God on our country.

Our Forefathers Were Not Saints

In English history there is the admission that the royals always made sure that the first male heir was legitimate. After that, anything might go and it didn't much matter whom the kings were bedding. Among American patriots, we know from history that Benjamin Franklin was a womanizer. Thomas Jefferson often visited "the quarter" where slaves were kept, as many other white slaveholders did. But since their slaves were chattel, property, they could beat them, sell them or have sex with their women. And they did. History has shown that progeny of Sally Hemings, a slave woman, were fathered by Thomas Jefferson. But so many Christians want to deny their history and make the founders of our country godly men. They were patriots. They were wise leaders. They may have even had the hand of God on their proceedings because there were praying Christians in their midst. But the ones we point to the most as our Founding Fathers were not necessarily men who yielded to the saving work of Christ in their lives.

When, after the country was launched, Jefferson and Adams were campaigning against each other for the presidency, they spoke terrible lies about each other. In the campaign of 1800, John Adams said that Jefferson "...was the son of a half-breed Indian squaw sired by a mulato father." That wasn't true but he said it anyway.

Jefferson said that Adams was a "...hideous freak of nature." He said that Adams was neither a man nor a woman. They told lies to get elected. Yet we point to these earlier times in our history as times of civility and gentlemanly behavior. We say that we would like to live in a country such as they formed. Politicians didn't lie back then as they do today, we like to say. Except that they did.

Our Fathers' God to Thee

Seminary student Samuel Francis Smith wrote the lyrics to the song "My Country, 'Tis of Thee" in 1831. Sung to the tune of "God Save the King," it was first performed at a children's program at Park Street Church, Boston, on July 4 of that year. We love the words, "Our fathers' God, to Thee, Author of liberty..."

Our Founding Fathers did speak of God in various ways, but as Jon Meacham tells us in his book *American Gospel,* "The Founders were aware that they were designing a government for a pluralistic nation—a country in which people of different faiths had to live together."

The Founders wrestled with words about God when forming the Bill of Rights. Some wanted specific references to God; others did not. The result was a document that allowed for religious freedom but did not establish one religion above another.

George Washington referred to "...that Almighty Being who rules over the universe." At his inauguration as the first president of the new nation he added at the end of his swearing in the words, "So help me God." Yet, according to historians, Washington would neither take communion nor kneel in prayer in spite of how later paintings depict him.

Samuel Adams, second cousin to John Adams, read the Bible each morning and attended weekly church services. Thomas Jefferson had a Bible too, but it was one in which he excised out all of the passages with which he did not agree. He preferred to refer to "nature's God" and was himself described as a mix of Deism, Unitarianism and Anglicanism. Even Abraham Lincoln, who along with George Washington is revered perhaps more than any other president, was criticized for not being a church goer. Historian William J. Wolf tells us that Lincoln was said to be "a scoffer of religion."

Some modern authors have written books about the faith of those who founded our country. But these authors have to do it by piecing together words such as "Nature's God" and "Creator" and make them sound more Christian than they were intended to be. That's not honest. We cannot make those long dead to be more Christian than they admitted to themselves.

Yet, because there is a God-shaped place in all of us, neither Supreme Court rulings, petitions by the ACLU, nor even laws passed can change the inner desire in people for the God they long to know. We are not all Christians but we are not all pagans either. The vast majority of people, then as now, are people who long for God and want to see Him in their lives even if they don't accept the biblical view of God or His Son sent to redeem us.

Sometimes politicians and others have used God, or at least have tried to use Him. Business leaders caught in a scandal may refer to the forgiveness of God. God is never far from us. We know that God is ever present, and sometimes those who do not yet know Him show flashes of understanding about Him before going back to themselves and their own attempts at shaping their lives and destinies.

So if America has never truly been a city on a hill in either its past or present, neither has it been a totally pagan place without any reference to God. Most people have an American sense of religion that some writers and speakers have tried to make into a revelatory understanding of God by turning words about God into affirmations of faith in God. Then, when we start to think that we were once a Christian people, we will lament how far we have fallen from what we once were in our past—a past that never was.

We should know our history and the beliefs of those who formed our country. We need to be accurate about them, what they believed, what they didn't believe and what they could have put into our founding documents making the United States a Christian nation but yet chose not to do so. We show that we are not honest historians if we try to pretend that those early founders were men of God who were forming a Christian nation with principles from which we have now strayed.

America in Our Early Days

What was our country like at the time of the Revolutionary War when our independence from England was declared and we fought for separation?

On July 4, 1776, the signers of the Declaration of Independence pledged "our lives, our fortunes and our sacred honor." They committed their all. They knew that they could be hung for treason.

But not all colonial people agreed with them. Thirty thousand joined up to fight with the British troops. By war's end, sixty thousand people who felt that they could not turn against the established government fled to England, Canada, Jamaica or other lands held by the British. Even Ben Franklin's son William, who was the governor of New Jersey, moved to England, never to return.

Dr. J. Edwin Orr, a professor who taught at Fuller Theological Seminary, told us how bad things were in our country after the Revolutionary War ended. Many clergy had left; churches were closing; drunkenness was rampant; bank robberies were a daily occurrence; women weren't safe on the streets. Sexual immorality multiplied the number of illegitimate births and sexually transmitted diseases.

A poll taken at Harvard discovered not one single believer in the whole student body. At Princeton only two students were found who were Christians and only five who did not belong to a campus group called "The Filthy Speech Society."

There was a mock communion service at Williams College, anti-Christian plays were put on at Dartmouth and in New Jersey a Bible—a pulpit Bible probably—was taken from a church and burned in a public bonfire. One Episcopal clergyman wrote: "How many thousands…never saw, much less read, or ever heard a chapter of the Bible! Tens of thousands who never were baptized or heard a Sermon! And thrice Ten thousand, who never heard of the name of Christ, save in Curses. Lamentable is the situation of these people."

And it was lamentable. In general assembly the Presbyterians met to deplore the ungodliness of the people. One church hadn't received a young person into membership in 16 years. The Protestant Episcopal bishop of New York decided he was out of work so he took up other employment. Chief Justice John Marshall wrote to the Bishop of Virginia that the church was "too far gone ever to be redeemed." This is not the country that our "make believe" people like to think existed when it was a new nation.

But during that time there was a pastor by the name of Isaac Backus who addressed an urgent plea for prayer. Soon prayer meetings began to spring up everywhere and people were being converted by the hundreds of thousands. Bible preaching churches were filled again and holy living became a passion. This became known as the Second Great Awakening and it spread across the country for the next 50 years. That's the moral country that we became, and it came about not by politics but by prayer.

If we color our history to make the country more Christian than it was, then we also have to delete or erase from our history the wonderful intervention of God that came about in our nation as a result of passionate prayer.

Historian A. T. Pierson said, "There has never been a spiritual awakening in any country or locality that did not begin in united prayer."

Patriots who are believers pray for their country. And patriots who are believers take their citizenship seriously. We have biblical principles that guide our thinking and our voting. But do we always know what that means? Do we just assume that all people in our country have been Christian or at least moral ever since that Second Great Awakening? Do we know our history as it was or do we varnish it to make it what we want it to have been?

The Greatest Generation

Even in more recent years we have tended to forget or have colored our history. Rick Atkinson, writing in his World War II book *The Guns at Last Light,* talked about the prostitutes in the darkened British streets feeling for the indications of rank on an American soldier's uniform before deciding what to charge him for having sex with her. Atkinson wrote: "So many GIs impregnated British women that the U.S. government agreed to give local courts jurisdiction in 'bastardy proceedings'; child support was fixed at £1 per week until the little Anglo-Americans turned thirteen, and 5 to 20 shillings weekly for teenagers. Road signs cautioned, 'To all GIs: please drive carefully; that child may be yours.'"

The stories of the American soldier in liberated France were no better. And once into the Rhineland crimes worsened with thousands of courts martial. General Eisenhower wrote in his diary, "Disciplinary conditions are becoming bad." To subordinates he said, "The large incidence of crimes such as rape, murder, assault, robbery, housebreaking, etc., continues to cause grave concerns."

When George Patton wanted the new miracle drug Penicillin given to his troops who had contracted sexually transmitted diseases, Eisenhower put his foot down. He said "No!" The drug would be used for the thousands of battle-wounded soldiers, not for soldiers who got diseases for what they shouldn't have been doing in the first place.

One report from a 29th Division unit stated, "We're advancing as fast as the looting will permit." Entire houses were "liberated" from attic to cellar. And often what could not be carried off was smashed. It was anger at the Germans as much as greed; that feeling swept through other allied troops, Canadian and British as well.

Yet we think that such behavior is limited to our day—not back during the Second World War—because the people then were "The Greatest Generation." They were great; they did fight and die; they did all the good things that we give them credit for. But history also shows that there was the other side as well. They were like any person without the changed life that only Christ can bring. We do neither ourselves nor our biblical teaching any favors when we choose to live in a make-believe world about the way people were then or are now.

America came out of World War II a powerful nation. But it is always good to remember the words of John Adams who wrote, "Power always thinks it has a great soul." When we try to make our nation more Christian than it was, then we have to deny the decadence that was there and, even more important, the way faithful people prayed and how God answered their prayers. If we want to avoid praying for our nation today, if we simply want to assume that we should get back to what we were when our country was founded or even to be like some earlier generation, then we no longer need the intervening hand of God and we are no longer true to our Christian faith—we have adjusted both our history and our faith.

But if we are convinced that our nation needs prayer today just as it needed prayer in the past, and if we are convinced that God is as able to bring renewal today as He did back when Isaac Backus called believers to pray, then we need to be on our knees before God, not on our soapboxes bashing the people who don't want a God-centered country.

No Prophets, No Epistles, No Problems

Our Christian history tends to be rewritten to suit us as well. Rather than give a history lesson that takes us down through the centuries, including the need for a Reformation, we need only to go back to the Bible itself and the proclamations of the prophets and the writers of the epistles to the churches. Why were they written? What were the issues? Were the people of Israel always faithful to God? Or did they need to be reminded of who they were and what they were doing that was contrary to the wishes of God?

Has the church always been faithful to the teachings of Jesus? Have all who named the name of Christ followed Him? If they had, would Paul have written the strong letters that he addressed to the believers of his day?

Was there a better time "back then"? When the epistles in the New Testament were written, the teaching didn't come from the culture but because of it. The culture was decadent, debauched. It was far worse than anything we see around us today. When Paul wrote about marriage, for example, it was a radical departure from the cultural norm. Christians were different, and when we read about husbands and wives it was at a time when most men made prostitution a part of their worship and women were considered property.

Today we seem to want to believe that the early church was a mirror of society, something we need to emulate in our culture. But the early church lived totally in opposition to the ways of the culture. When we lecture our culture about needing to "go back to being Christian," we prove that we know neither our Christian truth nor the culture that was stood against in the earliest days of the church.

Remember the words of the apostle Peter? Was he living in a democratic society where every citizen had a vote and the people in political office were fair and just rulers? It was, in fact, a cruel, vicious time. People had few rights. Still, Peter warned, "Be subject for the Lord's sake to every human institution…for this is the will of God" (1 Pet. 2:13–15, ESV). Christians were to fear God and honor the emperor. And in that passage Peter explains why, and the good that comes from living in this situation as people who are free—free in a far greater sense than being critical and putting our own wishes and wills ahead of the larger plan that God has for His people.

As followers of Jesus we are a called-out people, not a reform-society people. People aren't able to live the Christian life without the empowering of the Holy Spirit. No amount of protesting or law-making will do what only the Holy Spirit can do when He controls a person's life.

The more we look at our Christian history and our American history without our rose-colored glasses, the more we will see the hand of God on the church and in our land—even, sometimes, in spite of us. We do no one any favors when we reduce both the country and the church to a nice place where nothing bad ever happened in the past and everyone was a faithful servant of God. Then we think that we are living today in the worst of times. Tell that to our Christian forebears who lived as faithful believers in their pagan cultures. Tell that to the believers in the early church. Tell it to the hearers of the prophets.

Only God Can Turn Things Around

The secular person knows American history too. He knows when we misrepresent what our country was like. But he probably doesn't know the work of God in answer to the prayers of God's faithful people. He doesn't know what the Second Great Awakening did for our nation. He doesn't have that touchstone to see how far we have drifted today.

When we know our church history, especially the parts that the secular person also knows, but still pretend that we were all wonderful and faithful and there were never any struggles, we can't show the transforming power of God.

If we won't admit to what was wrong back then, we can't point to what God did to turn things around for us as faithful men and women who turned to Him in repentance and pledged as Joshua did that "as for me and my house, we will serve the Lord."

Years ago, when the Nazis had invaded Holland, a watchmaker told his daughter, "No pit is so deep that God is not deeper still." Corrie ten Boom believed those words of her father even when she and the rest of her family were taken off to concentration camps during World War II, having been arrested for hiding Jews above their watch shop in Haarlem, the Netherlands.

If we are in a deep pit now in our country, we can recognize that God is able to pull any of us, including the entire nation, out of that pit. Even though most secular people don't recognize that the pit exists, or that they are in it themselves, we know it. Being in that pit, seeing how bad things are and how they seem to be getting worse, should cause us to recognize that we still have a great God to turn to. His arm is not shortened—never has been, never will be. However deep our pit, He is deeper still.

It's an Old Story

I listen to my Christian friends argue against anything that is new, such as President Obama's Affordable Care Act, better known as Obamacare. I hear Christians refer to it as socialism. But that kind of talk isn't new. Such talk is part of our American history.

When Franklin Delano Roosevelt brought in Social Security, people argued that the government was taking over the family. Since time began we have always taken care of our own, they said. The care of the elderly was always the responsibility of the family; that care didn't belong to Washington DC. Many labeled Social Security as a form of communism where the state takes care of the people.

When Lyndon Johnson introduced Medicare, the screams got even louder. It's socialism, we were told. The president is trying to make us like the European countries where the government makes sure that we have health care.

But something very interesting has happened. The same angry people who cried out against Social Security have grandchildren who shout, "Don't touch it! Social Security is an entitlement. I couldn't make it in my old age without it. It is my right as an American."

And what about Medicare? The most vocal people I know, who now cry "socialism" about Obamacare, once used the same word to describe President Johnson's proposal of Medicare. Today many of those same people, returning from an expensive stay in the hospital, tell me with great enthusiasm, "Medicare covered it all." Now that too has become a right, an entitlement that must not be touched in any way.

Socialism is what many conservative Christians call the Affordable Care Act. Like Social Security and Medicare before it, there are surely many flaws that need to be tweaked in the program. Rarely has anything come out of Washington fully workable the first time around. Many of my Christian friends don't even want to give the Affordable Care Act a chance. They don't want to see whether or not it will work. They cheer each time the House of Representatives votes to destroy the program, even though by the time the House had voted for repeal more than 40 different times and even tied it into a government shutdown to get it defunded, it was obviously becoming a hang-up for some in our country.

Many American Christians have forgotten what they said when those earlier programs came out and are busily opposing the current program. Conservative Christians, who tell the world that they are Bible believers, still keep coming down on the side of insurance businesses and not on the side of the sick people who are uninsured. They do not resonate with secular people who know what Jesus taught about the poor and even about the cup of cold water. The culture can quote that part of Scripture to us.

Don't Be Like Europe

My friends tell me that we must never go the route of Europe. So, being the kind of person I am, I ask them why? They reply that the health care is not as good there and people have to wait up to six months to see a doctor.

I can point to two personal experiences about that. One is from Scotland and the other from Canada. In Edinburgh, my wife tripped on the steps of Edinburgh Castle and got a gash under her eye. We took a taxi to the Royal Infirmary. Then, remembering what we had been told about "socialized medicine," we prepared ourselves to wait forever to see a doctor. It was a Sunday afternoon; surely the hospital would be short-staffed. But in just a few minutes we were called in to a treatment room where a young surgeon saw to Andrea's cut. He cleaned it and then stitched it so well that later, back home, her own doctor was impressed when she removed the stitches. There is only a small scar there. When I asked that doctor how I should pay, he told me that there was no charge. "But I'm not from this country," I said. "I'm from America." It doesn't matter, he said with a smile, and we were on our way.

My second example is about a Canadian friend who had many medical problems. He called me one day when I was living in Minnesota and told me that he was going to the Mayo Clinic. I went to see him. He said that the doctors in Canada told him that Mayo would be able to give him the best care. So they flew him to Rochester, Minnesota, in an air ambulance, and the national insurance paid for everything. My friend told me, "Roger, if I lived in the U.S. I'd be dead."

Ignorance Is Not Bliss

My friends who argue with me about our country's having the best health care in the world haven't looked at the charts. When it comes to longevity, we rank 33rd among other nations, even below Slovenia and Kuwait. How could others live so much longer if their healthcare is so bad? When we look at charts of health costs, we soar way above other industrialized countries. If we look at infant mortality, we now rank number thirty among the nations and are still slipping. Back in 1960 the U.S. ranked 12th in the world in infant mortality. In 1990 we had slipped to 23rd. Now we are number 30. Why is this true? "Save the Children" CEO Carolyn Miles explained that the problem is that so many die in the first 24 hours and that many of the bàbies born in the U.S. are immature. Women, especially poor mothers, aren't getting access to medical care.

In *TIME* magazine, December 2, 2013, we were told what happens if the ACA fails. According to author Nancy Gibbs, we will be "...a country that pays too much and gets too little from its health care system, whose costs, at nearly 18% of GDP, limit America's ability to grow and invest and compete globally. Compared with other developed countries, the U.S. has more uninsured, fewer doctors per capita and lower life expectancies."

Many Christians in America don't want national insurance controlling our health care but do want for-profit insurance companies controlling our health care. We want no restrictions put on drug companies by the Congress so there can be no collective buying of drugs. We pay top prices. I know that I have paid much less for the same drugs in other countries when I needed them, whether in England or elsewhere. In one case, when we were in Copenhagen on 9/11, we had to stay four extra days before the flying ban was lifted and we were allowed to fly home. Being in that country longer than I had figured on, I ran out of one of my prescriptions. I went to a pharmacy, described to the pharmacist what I was taking and she supplied what I needed. It was that simple and it was inexpensive.

We have been told that we aren't allowed to buy our drugs more cheaply from Canada because those drugs might be compromised, not safe. But they are the same drugs that we have, manufactured by the same pharmaceutical firms. I wasn't happy when I found out later that some of our "safe" drugs have been formulated in China

We point to the presidents and the royalty of developing countries coming to the U.S. for surgery because it is better and safer here. And it is better and safer than what their country offers. But many Americans are going abroad for health needs, including surgery, because there are other places in the world where the care is better and cheaper. It is a two-way street. One day I asked a missionary friend who serves in a poor country where he would go if he needed major surgery. Without hesitation this American missionary said, "I'd go to South Korea. That's where I would get the best care." In 2007, approximately 750,000 Americans went abroad for health care, including surgery where it was just as good or better than the surgery in the U.S. and much cheaper.

The British publication *The Economist* (October 5, 2013) stated, "Overhauling America's $2.7 trillion health sector is no easy matter. In the world's biggest economy nearly 50 million people, or one in seven, are uninsured. America spends 18% of GDP on health care. The people of Britain, Norway and Sweden, to name a few, spend half as much but live longer." Then, giving just one example, the publication shows, "Replacing a hip in America costs more than three times what it does in Britain."

The Economist marvels, "The furor over 'Obamacare' is baffling to the rest of the world. Most rich countries have universal coverage; developing countries are trying to introduce it. Yet in America, home to the world's biggest health system, the fight over insurance is vicious enough to bring government to a halt."

In Texas, where one-quarter of the population is not insured, the governor opposes the Affordable Care Act, and when volunteers tried to help people understand the Act, they found that some of the people there didn't know anything about it and others believed that it had been repealed.

People of God Need to Be People Who Know

Is one medical system better than another? Possibly not. That isn't the point of this. What is important is that we who are the people of God ought to know what is real and what is not, what is true and what is false. We hear the same opposing arguments used in the health care debate so often that we assume they are correct, as though repeating something often enough makes it true. It may not be true.

I was caught by an article in the *Calgary Herald*. One of the most outspoken people against the Affordable Care Act has been Sarah Palin. Yet, she told Canadians, as reported in the *Calgary Herald*, that when she was young, "We used to hustle on over the border for health care. I think, isn't that kind of ironic now? Zooming over the border, getting health care from Canada." She is right. It is ironic.

During her campaign for vice-president, Palin told how she and her husband had "...gone through periods of our life here with paying out-of-pocket for health coverage until Todd and I both landed a couple of good union jobs." She recalled times "...in our past when we didn't have health insurance and we know what other Americans are going through as they sit around the kitchen table and try to figure out how they are going to pay out-of-pocket for health care."

Why does this matter? Because most secular people I talk to are willing to do a little research, check out information on these matters and form their ideas based on good study. Too many

Christians I know are not willing to do that. So my secular friends can only shake their heads at my Christian friends who insist that they are right about health care without ever checking to see if what they are saying is true. If we don't know but insist that we do, how can we have an intelligent conversation with our secular friends about what is most important and really true—the Gospel of the Lord Jesus Christ?

"Moore" Confusion

When a devastating twister hit Moore, Oklahoma, in 2013, the two senators in that state were apoplectic. They had voted against federal relief for the victims of Hurricane Sandy on the East Coast. Now President Obama was offering the same aid to victims of the Oklahoma tornado. What to do? They couldn't accept the aid without being seen as hypocrites, but the need was so great that they couldn't refuse it either. So they figured out a plan that would confuse even their supporters, and they got away with it. They announced that the federal relief for the tornado victims in Oklahoma would go to deserving people. The aid that was offered to people hurt by Hurricane Sandy was going to people who were not entitled to it. One of the senators announced that the aid for the two disasters was "totally different."

These politicians shifted and sidestepped and did some verbal gymnastics and made the system work for them but fought against it for others.

Here We Go Again

Many years ago, near the beginning of the 20th century, the Federal Council of Churches (in 1950 it became the National Council of Churches) sought to influence the culture and the political power structure in the United States by emphasizing political and social change. These who were labeled "liberal

Christians" were so convinced that they could make the United States into a Christian country, in their century, that they even launched a magazine called *The Christian Century*.

According to Wikipedia, "The Century was founded in 1884 as *The Christian Oracle*, in Des Moines, Iowa, as a Disciples of Christ denominational magazine. In 1900, its editor proposed to rename it *The Christian Century* in response to the great optimism of many Christians at the turn of the 20th century that 'genuine Christian faith could live in mutual harmony with the modern developments in science, technology, immigration, communication and culture that were already under way.'"

The fundamentalists, as they were known at that time, said, "You can't create a Christian country through simply changing laws or political positions. People need to have changed hearts. You should be preaching the new birth, reconciliation with God and holiness, not power politics." In the years since, many people have left the mainline churches that had that agenda so that the churches left in the council today are only a small remainder of what they once were. They had forgotten who Jesus is and what He came to do. They focused instead on politics and changing the culture. Their intentions were good but their reasoning was not.

But today, these many years later, I see conservative, evangelical Christians trying to do the same thing that the Council of Churches tried to do more than 100 years before. We want to elect the right politicians who will create an America that we want to have through enacting laws that we insist must be passed. Any message that we once had about Jesus being the only way, the only truth, the only life, has been replaced or drowned out by our attempts to do today what the Council of Churches failed to do years ago. I can almost hear the liberal Christians saying, "Didn't you learn anything from what we tried to do? Don't you remember what you told us?"

When I listen in on a Conservative Political Action Conference (CPAC) gathering or listen to vocal evangelicals, I hear being advocated the very things that these same people would have fought against years earlier. Conservative evangelicals are becoming the new Council of Churches, seeking to change the country's morals and behavior not through the miracle of new birth but by the human pressure of political action.

No Middle Ground

There was a time in American history when voters elected people who would go to Washington to work together for the common good. Now we work to elect people who will follow the instructions of those who want the president to fail. We once recognized that there is value in having people in political office who would work through the give-and-take of debate and who were willing to surrender some points in order to gain others. But not anymore. We seem to want only politicians who are interested in fragmenting the country. We want extremists who will not bend no matter which side of the political aisle they are on. The result is gridlock.

As a follower of Jesus, I get pushed into extremist camps. I find that there is no middle ground allowed for me. My fellow believers hear me question something that I think is politically doubtful and immediately I am classified and shoved into an extremist camp on the opposite political side—a side that I never chose for myself.

I remember being criticized for going to Washington DC at the invitation of the then president. The first invitation to visit the White House came from Jimmy Carter. Andrea and I accepted the invitation and went. Upon our return I received the curled lip and the sneer, "You must be a Democrat." Some years later, an invitation to visit the White House came from Ronald Reagan.

Upon my return from that visit other people gave me the same sneering treatment, "You must be a Republican."

No one seemed to understand that the acceptance of an invitation by the president is exactly that. There is nothing unpatriotic about seeing the duly-elected leader of our country. Accepting an invitation isn't a political statement. But so many people would make it so. There is no place in their world for courtesy, respect for the office or even, it appears, for common decency.

Am I Liberal or Conservative?

Am I a liberal or a conservative? So much depends on what the label implies, especially to voters. That's what the citizens of South Carolina had to decide when former Governor Mark Sanford ran for Congress. He had been caught in a lie about visiting his Argentine mistress, telling others, including his wife, that he was hiking. Later he even violated a court order by visiting his children at his then ex-wife's home.

When Sanford campaigned for a seat in Congress, he listed himself as a conservative and his opponent as a liberal. Apparently the life of a person doesn't matter, only the label he wears. The "Conservative" label got him elected. Now his "soul mate," Maria Belen Chapur, tells Infobae TV in Buenos Aires, "When we're together, we live together. Partly in Washington, partly in Charleston." That seems to be acceptable to even the Christian voters as long as Sanford is "Conservative."

Two Camps or Four?

Depending on how I answer people when they make a political statement, I am immediately classified as either a flaming, leftist liberal or a right-wing Tea Party conservative. And that carries over into my biblical stance. If I don't totally agree with one side or the other, I'm not just a political or social liberal or conservative, I am a biblical liberal or conservative too. There is no middle ground, no balance.

But, in reality, there are not two camps only. There are at least four.

1. Biblically liberal—socially/politically liberal
This is a person who holds liberal views politically, socially and biblically as well.
2. Biblically liberal—socially/politically conservative
This is a person who is liberal biblically but tends to be more socially and politically conservative.
3. Biblically conservative—socially/politically liberal
This is a person who is biblically conservative but more socially and politically liberal.
4. Biblically conservative—socially/politically conservative
This is a person who is conservative biblically and also conservative politically and socially.

It isn't difficult to find people who fit each of these categories. What is difficult is to hear it said that if a person is socially and politically conservative then he must be a Bible-believing conservative Christian when he may not be. Or we hear it said that if a person is politically and socially liberal, he must therefore be a biblical liberal as well.

Today we seem to be in a state of war with far fewer people, including Christians, referring to themselves as moderates or centrists. We don't want to think of ourselves as being "balanced." For some that is no longer an admirable quality. We want to fight an enemy, even a fellow American. We look for secrets, hidden motives, demons under the bed, anything by which we may label a person an enemy and then attack that person whom we have labeled.

We seem to be far more comfortable writing someone off by shoving him into the box we have selected for him than to allow him to express his views and explain why he holds them. People whom we want to quickly dismiss with a label are not people we will engage with in meaningful conversation about the things of the country or of God.

It has been said that most of us are not all one thing or another. About ten percent are fixed in position number one and about ten percent in position number four. The rest of us are in various degrees or gradients of one of the middle two positions.

But people who are in number one and people who are in number four tend to do the same thing—they immediately want to put the other people, those who have some variation in their thinking and are really part of groups two or three, into either the first or the fourth camp.

There are vocal number fours who might accept number twos because they are socially and politically conservative but reject the number threes because they are more socially and politically liberal even though number threes are biblical conservatives.

So we send two messages. One is that it doesn't matter if you are a follower of Jesus; you are still an enemy because you have a different social or political view than I have.

Second, it doesn't matter if you are a biblical liberal so long as you agree with my conservative position socially and politically.

How did we, who want to serve the redeeming God, get ourselves classified as opposites of the gospel we proclaim? Nobody did it to us. We took the world's position that suited us and assumed that our worldly position was the Christian view and the opposite worldview was that of the unsaved. This is what so destroys our Christian witness; we have created that situation ourselves.

An Old Testament Warning

There is a warning in the prophecy of Ezekiel. We read:

> When I say to a wicked man, "You will surely die," and you do not warn him or speak out to dissuade him from his evil ways in order to save his life, that wicked man will die for his sin, and I will hold you accountable for his blood. But if you do warn the wicked man and he does not turn from his wickedness or from his evil ways, he will die for his sin; but you will have saved yourself. Again, when a righteous man turns from his righteousness and does evil, and I put a stumbling block before him, he will die. Since you did not warn him, he will die for his sin. The righteous things he did will not be remembered and I will hold you accountable for his blood. But if you do warn the righteous man not to sin and he does not sin, he will surely live because he took warning, and you will have saved yourself (Ezek. 3:18–21).

Does that still hold true? Will we someday want to argue with God and tell Him, "But, Lord, I did warn people; I told them that they had to vote Republican." Or, "Lord, I was trying to save our country and the people in it and I knew that the wrong politicians would not be biblical in their behavior but the right politicians would bring in Christian behavior." I wonder if God will then remind us of that warning He gave through the prophet Ezekiel so many years ago. I also wonder if He will remind us about why He sent his Son, because all have sinned and come short of the glory of God. The saving Christ is the only redeemer.

In some ways Christians can't help themselves. A brainwashing is going on. Although most conservative evangelicals will deny it, it is obvious to unbelievers who see us not as followers of the Bible that we insist is true, nor of the Christ whom we proclaim to be the only way of salvation, but as followers of human manipulators. We are seen as followers of those who have made us believe that proper behavior and proper laws will make us a Christian people without the redemptive work of Jesus.

A Second American Revolution

I hear it talked about enough to figure there has to be some reason for it. I hear vocal Christians picking up the comments of some Tea Party extremists who feel that if they don't get their way, America may face another revolution. I understand why the Tea Party politicians say that, but why are some vocal Christians talking that way too?

One Christian speaker said, "America is at war...a life and death struggle over whether the God of the Bible will continue to be acknowledged as the one true God, and Christianity as the true religion."

Is America fighting a war? Are we in a life-and-death struggle to make America Christian? Is it done by war or through the work and power of Jesus? Does the entire country have to acknowledge that God is the one true God and Christianity is the one true religion? Is Christianity meant to be the national religion of America? Will Christianity as the national religion change the country?

On September 28, 2013, Christian newspaper columnist Cal Thomas wrote in an editorial, "Dysfunctional government is bringing us closer to the choice faced by signers of the Declaration of Independence; 'When in the Course of human events, it becomes necessary for one people to dissolve the political bands which have connected them with another, and to assume among the powers of the earth, the separate and equal station to which the Laws of Nature and of Nature's God entitle them, a decent respect to the opinions of mankind requires that they should declare the causes which impel them to the separation.'"

The writer goes on to say, "Those causes are abundantly clear. It may be time to consider separating ourselves from what the Framers might have regarded as a government foreign to them, which has led to the extortion of its citizens."

Cal may be right, but not for the reason he states. With 99 percent of the people growing poorer while one percent of the people grow richer day by day, the next revolution, if there is one, probably won't be brought about by those who already have and are taking from others. Dukes, earls, kings and queens don't call for revolution—peasants do.

Such reasoning is mostly about moral behavior and the slippages that we have watched take place. But if our first revolution is any indication, another revolt in America won't change morals but will only exacerbate the moral problems we already have. But moral behavior seems to be limited to such things as sex, not greed—what offers opportunities for the rich to get richer while the poor get poorer. So it may be that we are near another revolution, but perhaps not for the reasons that the Tea Party people are thinking about.

Spare the Rich; Hurt the Poor

Christians tend to believe, because that's what Rupert Murdoch tells them via his media, that the poor on food stamps should just go out and work. One example used is that of "Lobster Boy," who says he has no intention of working and spends some of his $200 per month food assistance on fresh seafood. He becomes the face of all who are on food stamps, including the truly needy who are struggling to feed their families. Having helped at a food pantry, I know who comes in and why they are very grateful for the needed help.

The apostle James, brother of Jesus, asked, "What good is it, my brothers and sisters, if someone claims to have faith but has no deeds? Can such faith save them? Suppose a brother or a sister is without clothes and daily food. If one of you says to them, 'Go in peace; keep warm and well fed,' but does nothing about their physical needs, what good is it? In the same way, faith by itself, if it is not accompanied by action, is dead" (James 2:14–17).

Do we believe what James said? If we oppose helping the poor with government-handled assistance, will we then step up and take care of the needy ourselves? One Christian man said, "I don't have to give money to the needs of the poor through the church; I pay taxes for that." But when he said that, he was a staunch supporter of those in political circles who are the ones opposed to giving government help to the poor. So the right hand gives the job to the left hand but the left hand is buried in the person's own pocket.

I know well-educated people who can't find work, as hard as they try. They struggle, turn to SNAP, the federal food aid program for the poor, and keep looking for work. They are labeled as being no different than "Lobster Boy," when in reality they work just as hard or harder to find work as those who are already working.

In the U.K., a parliamentary elections poster read, "Let's cut benefits for those who refuse to work." That might apply in the U.K., but if we applied that in the United States we would have to start with members of Congress who freely feed at the public trough but refuse to do the jobs they were elected to do. One Texan wrote to *The Economist*, "So Fox News is appalled to discover a slacker who is taking government benefits and perfectly comfortable about doing nothing to earn them. I know where it can find 535 more."

Does Christian Morality Exploit?

We think of the "welfare queen" but not the oil magnates or agribusiness executives or bankers who receive all kinds of government benefits allowing them to pocket great profits. If we were to add up the numbers, the gifts to the top one percent of the population far exceed the help given to those who are the working poor. Christians can be heard criticizing the man who robs a convenience store of a few dollars, calling him a crook. But a convicted criminal, such as the former head of Enron who cost so many people their jobs and their futures, was considered a moral man, a church-going man, even one praised by President George W. Bush.

Those who oppose welfare, or any help such as food stamps, argue that government gives too much away. But those who say that are also the ones who are always looking at those poorer than themselves, not at those whose incomes keep rising incrementally, often with the help of huge government handouts, creating one of the biggest gaps between the rich and poor we have ever had in our country.

We hear, "Leave businesses alone and let them regulate themselves." Yet those who want to limit regulations are the same ones who create huge problems for our economy when their greed goes unchecked. No recession great or small was caused by the working poor. Nor is it the working poor who, unregulated, will pollute rivers, allow their factories to spew mercury and other chemicals into the air causing deaths not only among adults but among babies and young children.

When Christians support those who exploit, it is noticed. When Christians reject the poor, it is noticed. When Christians are comfortable with pollution in the air and the poisoning of aquifers so that someone can increase his personal profit, it is noticed. But when a Christian cares about the hurting and the dying, that is noticed too.

In 2002 the Cato Institute estimated that 93 billion dollars went to corporate welfare, about five percent of the federal budget. Are Christians doing the math when business giveaways can cost billions whereas help for the poor costs pennies by comparison? Are Christians looking at this upside-down world through the teachings of Jesus, or not?

Do We Care about Regulating Banks?

We are told that 70 percent of new jobs come from small or new businesses. But are banks lending to those businesses to enable more people to work? Or are they using the money they hold for wheeling and dealing on Wall Street where larger profits can be made? Simon Johnson, former chief economist of the International Monetary Fund and now Ronald A. Kurtz, Professor of Entrepreneurship at M.I.T Sloan School of Management, wrote in *The New York Times*, "The people who run global megabanks would rather fund them with relatively more debt and less equity. Equity absorbs losses, but these very large companies are seen as too big to fail—so they benefit from implicit government guarantees." He explained that, "A higher degree of leverage—meaning more debt and less equity—means more upside for the people who run banks, while the greater downside risks are someone else's problem…the taxpayer."

Johnson added, "The big banks swear up and down that to subject them to a tougher leverage requirement…would somehow derail the economic recovery or even crater the global economy. This is a complete fabrication."

Not pulling any punches, author Michael Snyder wrote about the banks gambling "recklessly." He says, "If they win on their bets, they become fabulously wealthy. If they lose on their bets, they know the government will come in and arrange for the banks to be bailed out because they are 'too big to fail.' Either they will be bailed out by the government using our tax dollars or… they will be able to 'recapitalize' themselves by stealing money directly from our bank accounts. So if they win, they win big. If they lose, someone else will come in and clean up the mess."

Congressman Alan Grayson wrote to Fed Chairman Ben Bernanke stating that there is still "…too much gambling with other people's money, by banks that are often regarded as too big to fail." He quotes Nobel Prize winner Eugene Fama who argued, "The simple solution is to make sure these firms have a lot more equity capital…so they are not playing with other people's money." Congressman Grayson quotes the U.S. Government Accountability Office that puts the most recent financial crisis as costing society $22 trillion.

In their book *The Bankers' New Clothes,* by Anat Admati and Martin Hellwig, the authors explain why bankers, who were bailed out by the government already, don't want to put money aside as a security or safety cushion to prevent another collapse. They want to keep gambling with other people's money. If they win, they gain a huge windfall. If they fail, they will be bailed out again.

In his review of the book by Admati and Hellwig, Martin Wolf, chief economic commentator at the *Financial Times* asks a good question. "Why might even so tiny an increase in the equity-funded proportion of the balance sheet be objectionable? The answer is that what is small to everybody else is huge to bankers. To them, a one-third increase in equity means a 25-per cent decline in return on equity. To bankers, ICBs tiny step was a big reduction in prospective returns and so in their own rewards." He adds, "If you think that running banks with so little loss-absorbing equity is crazy, you are right…It makes no sense to build either bridges or banks sure to collapse in the first big storm."

In the waning days of 2013 came the Volker Rule which, if enforced beginning in 2015, could force banks to absorb some of their own losses. Attempts by banks to water it down didn't work and five federal agencies adopted the rule. The rule should stop federally insured banks from gambling in the securities markets with taxpayers on the hook for their losses. Will banks find ways around it? One columnist wrote the next day, "Rest assured banks will find loopholes." One regulatory lawyer said, "…it remains to be seen how aggressively it will be implemented and enforced."

Do Christians care? What is more important to the followers of Jesus, the nation's people who are struggling to support their families or the personal profits of the nation's bankers? Will Christians still be seen as the people who want to allow banks to regulate themselves when doing that guarantees big profits for the shareholders but also risks another financial collapse causing the entire country to suffer and another bailout using the people's money?

Who Pays Taxes?

There was a famous saying by businesswoman Leona Helmsley that, "Only the little people pay taxes." She was right in one sense, but not in another. The disparity between top earners and lower wage workers gets ever larger. When a newspaper report showed that at McDonald's restaurants the average worker was earning $8.25 an hour, it also showed that the CEO of that company was taking home $8.75 million that year. When the newspapers pointed this out, McDonald's came out with a "budget" that showed workers how they could live on their low wages. Not only were the expenses unrealistic, the budget created by these top executives for their underpaid workers had nothing for heating and left out food and clothing. The sample "budget" was totally out of sync with reality but did show that those at the top have no understanding of those at the bottom. Besides the budget that earned derisive laughter from the media, it was noted in a Bloomberg report that the company did have enough money to hire lobbyists to fight against any increase in the minimum wage.

According to Bloomberg, 20 years ago the CEO of McDonald's was earning about 230 times what a full-time employee of that company was earning. Today it is about 580 times greater. An employee would have to work a million hours, or 100 years, to earn what the CEO is paid in one year. Even then that employee wouldn't have the perks of annual physical exams, a company-provided car for his personal use, and use of the company aircraft for personal trips.

But that CEO is not alone. HUFFPOST reports that top-tier CEO pay grew nearly 15 times faster than worker pay from 2011 to 2012. "The median pay of a CEO at a company in the Standard & Poor's 500 stock index rose by nearly 20 percent from 2011 to 2012, according to a new report by the research firm GMI ratings. In contrast, the median weekly earnings of full-time wage and salary workers rose by just 1.4 percent in the same period, according to data from the Bureau of Labor Statistics." Then we are told, "The U.S. leads the developed world in income inequality."

Meanwhile the country has to get by with fewer tax payers and lower tax payments. The superrich, like Leona Helmsley, know how to hide their income so that it won't be taxed. The low-wage earner doesn't have a large enough income to pay much in taxes. Two things are happening. First, infrastructure building and repairs are not being done so that roads, bridges, sewers, etc., are neither getting repaired nor rebuilt. Second, the people who buy the goods that make manufacturing strong don't have the money to buy those goods. A simple example from the past explains the point.

When Henry Ford started manufacturing automobiles at an ever-increasing rate because of the production line, cars were rolling out of the Ford plant in large numbers. But who would buy those cars? Ford knew what others didn't. He raised the wages of his factory workers to five dollars a day—a huge increase over what workers elsewhere were making at that time. The workers got higher wages and with those higher wages were able to buy the Ford cars that were pouring off the assembly line.

But today, the gap between the high-end executives who can hide their money from taxes and the low-end workers who don't earn enough to pay much in taxes is increasing. Neither can the low-end workers buy the products that are being produced.

In her column (*TIME* magazine, September 9, 2013), Rana Foroohar wrote about the huge cash stockpiles companies have but won't use for research and development, preferring the short-term profits for stockholders. She writes, "Wall Street places huge pressures on firms to act in ways that maximize short-term profits at the expense of long-term job-creating investments." This creates both a richer class and a poorer class. She explains, "Many economists believe that inequality can ultimately slow growth in an economy like ours, which is 70 % dependent on consumer spending." She quotes University of Texas economist James Galbraith who points out, "…as asset markets get bigger, inequality does too." So, Foroohar points out, "Apple which has some 147 billion in cash on hand (and $3 billion in profit rolling in every month)," is borrowing money. Why? "It doesn't want to repatriate the cash it has in overseas accounts and be forced to pay U.S. tax rates on it." This, the writer explains, "…has allowed U.S. firms to shoulder a smaller share of the country's tax burden over the past 30 years, even while corporate profit as a share of GDP has been rising."

If, as Cal Thomas hints, there is going to be another American revolution, it probably won't be the one the Tea Party people are thinking about. Who among the rich will rebel against what is for them an ideal world? When poor people can't take any more, they are the ones most likely to rebel, and those over them won't understand why. Before the American Civil War, any slaveholder would have said, "My slaves are happy." But everyone knows that they weren't happy at all. Has anything changed?

Are We Supporting the Oppressors?

If Christians want to support those who are seen as the oppressors, they won't be on the side of history. And a reading of Scripture, especially the teachings of Jesus, shows that siding with the ones who hurt others is not something that is smiled upon by God. If we who are Bible-believing Christians want to have any witness to our society and nation, we need to pay more attention to Jesus or we will increasingly lose our voices.

In our history we see that Christians built hospitals because people were suffering. Christians built colleges and universities because they knew that an educated people would be able to read, including their Bibles, and make a strong and viable contribution to society.

Social scientists do not deny that Christian people tend to donate more than others to charities, even to secular charities for cancer research, helping wounded veterans or to combat AIDs. They cheat less, make better and more honest workers and often help others more than secular people do. It is the Christians who do so much to help generate the kind of social capital that brings good to others.

If Christians today would not veer into extremism, being known for our strident demands that others live the way we want them to live, but instead become followers of Jesus on His terms, we can once again do what the early Christians did and present His teachings and His love to the people around us. Then our Christian history, as well as our American history of which we are rightfully proud, will not be lost in the cacophony of strident voices that, in the name of Jesus, are making us seem like anti-patriots who only want to baptize the secular culture rather than bring people to see and want the Savior who changes lives for His sake and ours. Until then, we may continue to be seen as people who follow the propagandists of our day rather than Jesus—and lose our Christian witness to those people who are still wandering in darkness.

Yet we still have an opportunity to follow Jesus as faithful disciples and to demonstrate His love to others. We have wonderful opportunities to reach out to secular people and help them to understand the saving work of Jesus. Some Christians wonder, "How can I explain the Savior to those who are locked into their secular world?" There are ways to do that. We will examine some of those ways next as we look at answers to questions that come from those who challenge us.

chapter 6

Presenting Good News to Secular Minds

I remember Ken. He made such an impression on me that I wrote about him in the December 10, 2011, issue of the *War Cry*. When World War II broke out Ken was just old enough to fly for his native England. He was stationed on an aircraft carrier in the Mediterranean, flying the double-winged "Swordfish" with its single torpedo. It was dangerous work. I asked him one day, "Ken, did you ever hit a ship with a torpedo?" He replied, "Yes, one, and then that ship got me."

Had someone been praying for Ken when he was in the war? He survived, and when the war ended he moved to the United States. In New York, he began a career in the book publishing field that took him to the top ranks of executive management. He had it all—the money, the houses, the yachts. But he didn't have Christ.

I met Ken when he was 82 years old. As I watched the next two years go by, I would often speak to him about his soul. He usually tried to deflect my conversations to something less personal. But still, he welcomed my visits. I did learn that he had never, ever, prayed for himself. Nor, as far as he knew, had anyone ever prayed for him. I told him I was praying for him and he began to let me pray for him aloud when we were together. Often I prayed the truths of the salvation-centered Scriptures, connecting those words to Ken's name.

Age took hold of Ken as one year passed to the next and he became weaker; finally, he was hospitalized. In the hospital I asked him again about his soul and discussed with him where he stood with the Savior. Then, one day, in the hospital, he was suddenly ready. That day he prayed to invite Jesus into his heart and life. After I prayed for him, he prayed his own words aloud. I knew that it was the first time in his life that he had ever done that. He ended his prayer with the words, "And I want you to take over my life."

Ken lived for three more months. The last time I saw him, in hospice, he was being visited by another acquaintance. So I said to this other man, "You know Ken is a follower of Jesus now." I will never forget what Ken said next.

He replied, "Yes, and these have been the happiest three months of my life."

Ken died days later. He is in heaven now. But he stayed on earth long enough after his decision for Christ to teach me a lesson. The years may go by; I may wonder if someone I am praying for who considers himself to be a secular, nonreligious person will ever come to saving faith. But then I remember Ken.

God doesn't stop reaching out, offering His saving love. Years may come and go, a person may seem locked in his unbelief, but God never quits. And I have learned from talking with Ken that God may be at work in ways I do not see. This man, who seemed to have it all, didn't really have it all—he knew it and God knew it. What God was doing in Ken's heart was not observable by me any more than a farmer can see what is happening to a seed under the ground until a new shoot pops through to the sun.

I don't know who might have prayed for Ken when, as a young man, he went off to war. But I'm convinced that surely somebody did. More than 65 years later, that person's prayer was answered. How many years will it take before other secular men

I am praying for come to the end of themselves and yield to God who is ever seeking them? I may not live long enough to find out. But that doesn't matter.

I'm the one who measures the passing years. God, who created time, doesn't. I'm the one who looks at what seem like wasted years. But God has never rescinded that promise to the prophet Joel, "I will restore to you the years that the swarming locust has eaten" (Joel 2:25, KJV).

I will keep on trusting that others for whom I've prayed so many years will someday say with conviction, "These years, months or even days have been the happiest of my life." In our secular culture, in our world where we wish people would act like Christians, we have what others need. We don't criticize them for what they don't have, we don't blame them for living in darkness; we bring to them the light of Christ.

Not Closed but Searching

People are searching; they are looking for meaning. Ravi Zacharias, who enjoys interacting with intellectuals, says in his book, *Can Man Live without God?* "In searching for ourselves, we can never know ourselves until we know him." When we help people to know Christ, they will also come to know the value of themselves. Ravi Zacharias goes on to say that "…sin robs us of our true nature and denies us the vision of who we really are."

The Trappist monk Thomas Merton said, "Man is not at peace with his fellow man because he is not at peace with himself. And he is not at peace with himself because he is not at peace with God." Is there anybody in my world who is not at peace with himself? They are all around me.

And one more quote: philosopher, mathematician and physicist, René Descartes (1596–1650), said, "…the idea of a perfect mind must have been planted in the imperfect mind by the perfect mind itself—which has to have been God." He was arguing that the idea of God as Infinite Being could not occur in the finite mind of a human being unless God really existed. The idea of God as Infinite Being is an innate idea in the human mind, an idea which cannot be created by any finite being. This perfect idea can be created only by God.

God has placed within our imperfect minds the desire to know the Perfect Mind. Our job is to be Good News tellers who can point people to the Perfect Mind, the Mind that the apostle Paul reminds us was in Christ Jesus.

In his own thinking, the secular person is basically good. It is society that is bad. In the Christian understanding, "…all have sinned and come short of the glory of God." In God's mind we are not simply sinners but we are dead in our trespasses and sin. We have to know that when we approach a secular people with the Good News of new life in Christ, we are approaching those who rarely see that sin in themselves. A person may be spiritually dead but he doesn't know it. Our job is to be spokespersons for the One who brings forgiveness and life.

When we help people come to fullness and peace in Christ, we are helping incomplete people come to completion and dead people to find the One who gives life—the abundant life here and the continuing eternal life that never ends. The only question for each of us is, "Will I be a Good News bringer about God's peace or will I keep bringing only political or social information that has nothing to do with a person's deepest need and nothing to do with the Gospel of life?"

How Will I Reply?

There are so many positions that people around take that form the basis for their own chosen way of life. Here are some of them:

1. "I have my own philosophy."

2. "I have always tried to live by the Golden Rule."
3. "My church membership means a lot to me."
4. "There are so many religions. Each person thinks his religion is right."
5. "You quote from the Bible, but the Bible is full of contradictions and errors."
6. "Aren't you being rather narrow stating that Jesus is the only way to God?"
7. "I have met too many nasty and hypocritical Christians."
8. "I believe in heaven. I don't believe in hell. How can a loving God…?"
9. "I'm not religious."
10. "Religion has caused so much trouble and pain in the world. We would be better off without any religion."

"I have my own philosophy."

Many people who live around us do have their own philosophy or self-made religion. In fact we live in a time of cafeteria religion and other beliefs where each person decides for himself what he wants to believe or not believe and the philosophy he creates for himself to follow. This can be very comfortable. Their religion or philosophy of life suits them. There is nothing in their belief system that corrects or contradicts them.

When engaged with an unbeliever, I always ask that person, "Tell me about your philosophy." It is important that I hear him. I can't expect a meaningful conversation if I don't hear what that person is saying about what guides his thinking and his life. In my heart I know what God says: "For my thoughts are not your thoughts, neither are your ways my ways, declares the LORD. As the heavens are higher than the earth, so are my ways higher than your ways and my thoughts than your thoughts" (Isa. 55:8–9).

Or, if I want to gently give that person something to think about beyond his own religion or philosophy, I will ask some of the same types of questions that God asked Job: "Where were you when I laid the earth's foundation? Who marked off its dimensions? Surely you know! Have you ever given orders to the morning, or shown the dawn its place...? Have you journeyed to the springs of the sea? What is the way to the abode of light? Do you send the lightning bolts on their way? Do they report to you...? Who endowed the heart with wisdom or gave understanding to the mind?" (Job 38:1–36).

The key is to explore that person's philosophy or his own religious beliefs because chances are he has never had to explain what he believes. Too often Christians either run away or become aggressive and defensive. It is better to pull out of him what he thinks. Being a learner helps us to understand but also helps him to explain what he may never have had to really explain before.

Exploring and voicing his religion or philosophy will very often reveal to him the holes in what he thinks he believes and what he has followed all of his life. By my not becoming defensive, and by drawing him out, he has to look more deeply at his own philosophy. Often, when that happens, a person soon explains away his own self-created convictions because in explaining them he sees that they don't tie together logically. There is a lot of blind faith required in man-made religions or self-created philosophy.

"I have always tried to live by the Golden Rule."

I can agree with that person. He has probably tried hard to live that way and needs to be commended for it. Often I say, "I see in you a kind and generous person." That's not hard to say because it is true—he is a kind and generous person. Sometimes people with their own personal view of God, their own philosophy of life, do better with the Golden Rule than many Christians. I need to let him see that I respect him for the good way he has lived his life.

But I also know and can point out that the apostle Paul (formerly Saul) was a religious man who kept the Jewish law. He had a strong belief system that guided his life. But when Paul met the Messiah he had to admit, "...not because of righteous things we had done..." (Titus 3:5). And, "For it is by grace you have been saved, through faith—and this not from ourselves, it is the gift of God—not by works..." (Eph. 2:8–9).

If our own good behavior was enough to satisfy the One who is Holy and totally Other, would Jesus have had to come for us? Would He have needed to go to the cross for us? If there are other ways to reach out to God, why doesn't God accept those other ways? But clearly God states many times in many ways that He does not. God's statement is clear: "This is my Son, whom I love. Listen to him!" (Mark 9:7).

If my exemplary behavior is good enough—in my opinion, not God's—and I go to God with that behavior to tell Him that I merit the good gifts of God, including eternal life, what will I say when he points to His Son and asks, "What have you done with Jesus?" Will I say, "Oh, You don't understand; I believe I'm good enough by my own merits and by my own definition of what is good"? Or will I say, "I've made myself eligible for heaven by my own good works; I don't need Jesus even though You keep telling me that I do"? Or will I say to God, "It doesn't matter what You tell me; I think my own way is the correct way"?

Articulating those disagreements with God will probably be new to the person who depends on his own good behavior. Many haven't even realized that they have been spending their lives telling God that what He says is wrong and what they say is right. Many have simply assumed that a person's own way of following the Golden Rule will be satisfactory to God even though God clearly states the opposite.

I can present those thoughts to a person who has his own religion or philosophy of life and who is trying to live by the Golden Rule on his own terms and in his own strength. Are we willing to trust in the philosophy or religion we have created for ourselves when God offers us His own way through Christ? Will we keep walking away from God while all the time insisting that we are right or will we turn around and, perhaps for the first time in our lives, honestly face God on His terms? Will we continue to trust in our own good works while telling God that His statements about our works can't possibly be right?

"My church membership means a lot to me."

Even though church membership in the U.S. seems to be declining, especially among the mainline denominations, even those who choose to go to church may be choosing to do so for reasons other than what scriptural Christianity refers to when it talks about the church, the body of believers. A church relationship can be cultural more than Christian, or be based on "what I get out of it" more than the worship of God and growth in Christian discipleship.

A man recently told me that he has been a member of his church for 45 years. Yet as I spoke about Jesus and why He came to save us, the man interrupted me with, "Well, I'm not focused on Jesus." In another church the members are thrilled with their minister's dramatic ability in the pulpit and his broadminded acceptance of many "truths."

I once served as a youth pastor in a Baptist church in New York. One day I told the pastor that one of the young men in the church had just asked Jesus to be his Savior. The pastor stared at me with a blank look and then replied, "Well, I suppose that's all right. But won't he get the idea that he is better than the others?"

If a person is depending on his church connection to be his means of pleasing God, he may not realize that Jesus had harsh things to say about those who were the most religious people of his day. He called them hypocrites. When my secular friends mock religious people as hypocrites, I remind them that they are in good company; Jesus said the same thing. I tell them that if they are going to talk about religious hypocrites they will have to get in line behind Jesus. And, with tongue in cheek, I will sometimes add, "Of course we all know that there are no hypocrites in business or on Wall Street or among Washington politicians." I don't usually have to say anything more.

There are many church people who are sincere, genuine in their convictions, but who may or may not understand what Christian truth is. Just as I've met many believers in every denomination, I've met many in every denomination who have no idea why they need to be converted.

I can reply to the "my church" people with their early church history, the basis of its foundations, especially the creeds and what those creeds say. Some people have repeated those creeds every Sunday for years without understanding what they mean. The same is true of many of the historic written prayers or the great hymns of the church. They point to God's saving work in Christ, but many who repeat them or sing them don't know that. They just say or sing words.

I will often refer to someone in that person's denomination who is a strong follower of Jesus. It may be someone quite well known in that church. That person I point to knows full well that his church membership doesn't save him. I can show how that church leader, who is strong in their denomination, isn't trusting in his church for salvation; he is trusting in the Son of God who came to save.

When I am speaking with my Roman Catholic friends, they seem surprised when I tell them that I was once invited to give the homily in a Roman Catholic Church. For years I kept a Bible with the imprimatur of their church on it. Many of my Catholic friends were more comfortable with looking at what the Bible says about salvation in Christ alone if they could read the words in a text that had been sanctioned and approved by their church. Sometimes I would turn to those familiar words in Acts 4:12 where Peter says, "Neither is there salvation in any other for there is no other name under heaven given among men whereby we must be saved." I don't have to remind my hearers that these are the words of the man they call their first pope.

In Minnesota I knew about a faithful Roman Catholic lady named Rose Totino who had a business that was later purchased by Pillsbury. One day she was driving in her car and listening to Christian radio when the speaker explained the clear message of salvation. She pulled to the side of the road and surrendered her heart to Christ. It was her Damascus Road experience. She went on to give major support to Christian ministries but always remained faithful to her Roman Catholic Church because there were other believers there and because, as she explained, for an Italian Catholic family, the church is part of their life and culture.

"There are so many religions. Each person thinks his religion is right."

When I meet a person who says that to me, I like to reply with, "You must be reading the Bible; you are quoting Scripture." The Bible tells us, "There is a way that appears to be right, but in the end it leads to death" (Prov. 14:12).

There are many religions and all have followers who believe they are right. We are a very religious people. That's understandable. God made us with a need for Himself. We will either respond to Him as He reaches out to us or we will try to reach out to Him in our own way, but we will do something to seek to fill that void in the soul that God has placed within us. Augustine said, "You have made us for yourself, and our hearts are restless, until they can find rest in you."

Restless hearts will find God on His terms or they will create a god they can reach on their own terms. There is no such thing as faith and non-faith. We will place our faith in God or in something else, but we will live by faith.

There were certainly a lot of religions when Jesus came. He never tried to explain them all away. That is quite fruitless and there is no point in our trying to do it either. Even when Jesus was conversing with the Samaritan woman at the well and she tried to sidetrack him with a theological argument, He brought her back to her own spiritual thirst and clearly explained to her that He is the water of life. "…whoever drinks the water I give them will never thirst" (John 4:14). We all have a spiritual thirst. Some who deny it demonstrate their thirst in ways they might not see but that others see in them.

There are many religious people who are still thirsty. Religion, which comes from man himself, can never satisfy a thirst that only God can satisfy. In their honest moments, people know they are spiritually thirsty and some even realize that their thirst is for God. They can come to the One who quenches thirst or, as the Bible shows us, they can dig "…their own cisterns, broken cisterns, that cannot hold water" (Jer. 2:13). It helps to ask a person when he thinks he will stop digging those broken cisterns.

"You quote from the Bible, but the Bible is full of contradictions and errors."

I always light up when I hear someone say that. I'll usually reply, "Oh, good. I am so glad to be talking with you. For years I've heard people talk about contradictions and errors in the Bible but I have been reading the Bible for a long time and I can't find those contradictions and errors." Then I'll take out my New Testament, which is often in my pocket, and hand it to him, asking, "Will you show me the contradictions and errors that you've found?"

Usually the person's hands will come up defensively and he starts to back away, stuttering that he couldn't pick something out right then. So I'll ask if he will look them up at home and call me. But he doesn't. And I know that he can't.

He has probably never been asked before to point out the contractions and errors that he is certain are in the Bible. Too many Christians get worked up and defensive about God's Word. When Christians do that, it convinces a person that he must be right and that the Bible does have contradictions and errors. He doesn't know any, but it must be true because of the reaction of people who claim that the Bible is true. He doesn't have to say any more.

We don't have to defend the Bible; we only have to bring the words of the Bible to someone's attention. The word of God is "…alive and active. Sharper than any double-edged sword…" (Heb. 4:12). It does its own work. I don't have to help the Bible.

I'm comfortable with the Word of God. It has proven itself true to me for many years. Before I became a Christian, I too used the "contradiction and errors" argument because that's what I'd always heard. But when I came to faith, I started reading the Bible. The more I read, the more the light came on. Even when some passages were beyond me, I could read what others taught about those parts of Scripture. Or, once I started looking at the context of the passage, the setting and what was said before and after a certain text, its truth bore out. If I were to take the Bible out of context, pasting together a verse here and there, I might be able to create a "contradiction." But I can't do it if I read what the Bible says based on trying to understand it, not trying to disbelieve it.

I've also heard arguments about the Bible's having been written by people many years after events happened, especially the New Testament. But if those who say that would read historians, they'd find that their assumption isn't true. History points to early, not late, writings of the Scriptures. There were enough people around with good memories of Jesus who could have refuted the New Testament writings if there was anything untrue about them.

One of my masters' degrees is in journalism from Michigan State University. I wrote my master's thesis on "Luke, Journalist of the New Testament Church." I had to defend my thesis before a secular committee at that university. I did my research and could show that Luke recorded what he experienced and saw. The degree that was granted also brought me into Kappa Tau Alpha, an honors society that recognizes academic excellence and promotes scholarship in journalism and mass communication. Honest secular scholars will recognize what is true and what isn't. We only have to be accurate and faithful to Scripture when we present it to others.

"Aren't you being rather narrow stating that Jesus is the only way to God?"

Being broad-minded is sort of the in thing for anyone who wants to be critical of the Christian faith. But being broad-minded isn't welcomed anywhere else. Who wants a broad-minded brain surgeon who prefers to believe what he chooses to believe about my tumor and ignores prescribed procedures for removing it?

Who wants to be on an airplane with pilots who each want to do things their own particular way? They may feel that instructions from the tower are only suggestions, one of many options. Even scientists are not broad-minded. A chemical can't be whatever he wants it to be. The same is true for mathematics. There are fixed teachings. The person doing math doesn't have the option to make an equation be whatever he would like it to be. And even when I watch a baseball game, I don't want broad-minded umpires for whom the strike zone is whatever they want it to be, with their choice changing in each inning.

I don't mind admitting that I am narrow. I follow the One who said, "Enter through the narrow gate. For wide is the gate and broad is the road that leads to destruction, and many enter through it. But small is the gate and narrow the road that leads to life, and only a few find it" (Matt. 7:13–14).

There is a broad way that many have chosen to travel. They've made a choice. It isn't my choice and I wish that it wasn't their choice, but if they choose the broad way and I don't, they can't justify their choice by declaring that I am narrow. I remember someone joking one time about his sister. He said, "She is so open-minded that her brains are going to fall out."

I have made a choice to go the narrow way toward life. Jesus is the gate, and there is only one gate that He offers. That gateway is Jesus Himself.

"I have met too many nasty and hypocritical Christians."

So have I. In fact, I look at one every day in the mirror. I can honestly say with the apostle Paul that "…I have the desire to do what is good, but I cannot carry it out. For I do not do the good I want to do, but the evil I do not want to do—this I keep on doing (Rom. 7:18–20).

But I can also lay claim to the rest of what the apostle said, "What a wretched man I am! Who will rescue me from this body that is subject to death?" (Rom. 7:24). The apostle turns to the only one who can free him: the Lord Jesus Christ.

Frankly, as painful as it is, I'm glad that the hypocrites are in the church where they can get help. And I will remind the person making the charge about hypocrites in the church that he has probably never met a hypocrite anywhere else. It usually doesn't take long before the person will back off and say, "Well, yes, there are hypocrites everywhere."

Then I will often ask that person to tell me about a hypocritical Christian who stands out in his mind. Often, once he has gotten it out of his system and recognizes that he may have been excusing himself by holding onto that example for many years, he is ready to come back to where he is himself in his relationship with Christ.

I can agree with him that there are professing Christians who don't seem to be following Jesus. They may have never really come to a saving experience with Christ and are Christian in name only, or they may truly be Christians but haven't grown in their faith. We are products of our genes, our surroundings, our education, our experiences, and we are shaped by them. God can remake us but we must be willing to let Him do that remaking.

There are well-meaning sledgehammer Christians, ill-tempered nasty Christians, shady political Christians and Bible-twisting Christians. All need the healing, correcting and changing power of the Holy Spirit. It's good if they are in a fellowship of believers who can teach them and pray for them. But while they are still on the way, they can make life difficult for others.

The early church was made up of believers who were shaped and pulled and influenced by many things, including the culture around them. The New Testament epistles are evidence of all that professing Christians got themselves into that was wrong. If those early Christians had been perfect, the epistles to the churches might have been different.

Even the disciples of Jesus did not always behave as men I would admire. They show what people are but also what they can be when transformed by the resurrected Christ. Peter was not an admirable follower of Jesus on the night of the betrayal. But he became a faithful man of God after he met the risen Christ. Then he became strong in the faith and his convictions stayed with him right to death. There may be a lot of people like Peter in our churches who are not yet what they are going to be. Until then, some will point the finger and call out "hypocrite."

"I believe in heaven. I don't believe in hell. How can a loving God...?"

We like heaven; we don't like hell. So we choose to believe in heaven but we choose not to believe in hell. After all, it is all about my choice anyway, isn't it? There are people all around us who believe this. They want a god who is like a benevolent grandfather, so they create one. They want a god who does only what they want him to do, so they fashion one; that god usually sounds just like them. They don't want a god who might not swing wide the door to heaven for them. Those kinds of made-up beliefs are very convenient.

But if we believe that God reveals Himself through Christ and the word, if we believe that when the Scriptures were given they came, as the apostle Peter explained, "For prophecy never had its origin in the human will, but prophets, though human, spoke from God as they were carried along by the Holy Spirit" (2 Pet. 1:21), then we have to put aside our own created ideas about Scripture and pay attention to what God says about Himself.

Since everyone knows what it is to work for a living, I will often show a person the words that explain how we earn our judgment; it is an effort we make to earn it. The Bible is clear, "For the wages of sin is death" (Rom. 6:23). We work for death and we earn what we work for. If I work for death, why am I surprised if that's what I earn? If I roll up my sleeves, apply myself to sin and its resulting death, why should I be given something other than what I have worked so hard to earn?

The Scripture is clear about sin. I am a sinner, based on God's definition of sin as measured against who He is in His holiness. God cannot look at sin; He has said so. The ancient Hebrew prophet Habakkuk said, "Your eyes are too pure to look on evil; you cannot tolerate wrongdoing" (Hab. 1:13). So why does it surprise anyone that God isn't going to somehow forget all of that which I have worked so hard to achieve—death? I may not mind my sin, but God does. And there is a reason. He knows where it leads; He knows how it destroys us and those around us. The nature of sin is that it will work itself out in acts of sin and take us to eternal death. God knows that.

Sin leads to death. We have worked hard to earn those wages and we are paid the wages we've earned. We can't work for our wages and then demand of God, "Why did you pay me these wages?" And, there is another part to this. When we read on in Romans 6 we find the rest of that passage. It reads, "...but the gift of God is eternal life in Christ Jesus our Lord" (Rom. 6:23).

What can we do to earn a gift? We can accept a gift or we can reject a gift, but we can't earn a gift. God offers us the gift of forgiveness and life. If we reject His offer, why do we complain that we don't have what He offered? If someone offers me a gift and I slap it away, I can't then blame that person because the gift isn't in my hand.

The good news is that God has always been reaching out to those who refuse His gift of forgiveness and life. In spite of us, we read what God said, "I am the LORD, the God of all mankind. Is anything too hard for me?" (Jer. 32:27). And nothing is too hard for God. Not even my stubborn heart.

People have always sought liberty, as if they are better off when "free" of God. Then, when the troubles come, and they always do, these same people complain, "So where was your God when all these bad things happened to me?" We hurt ourselves when we choose death over life and work hard for that death. We can rail at God for what we think is unfair about those things that are happening to us. Yet God still pleads, "I take no pleasure in the death of anyone, declares the Sovereign LORD. Repent and live!" (Ezek. 18:32).

God takes no pleasure in the death of those dying without eternal life, but He takes much pleasure in those who are heading toward heaven and a life that never ends. We read, "Precious in the sight of the LORD is the death of his faithful servants" (Ps. 116:15).

In the face of all this, will I still tell God, "No, I won't" when asked to accept His gift of life and then curse Him because "You have no right to let me go to hell"? We want our way, but we want God to not let us face the consequences of demanding our own way. Still, I meet many people who don't want God, don't want His offer of life, don't even want to admit that God exists but who will still say, "How could your God allow…"

"I'm not religious."

A man sitting in the seat next to me on a plane asked me what I did for a living. When I told him, he pulled away saying, "Well,

I'm not religious." I replied, "I'm not either." He really didn't want to talk anymore so I simply explained why I am not religious. I figured that if I could leave him thinking about religion and the Christian faith, that would be worthwhile. I didn't want to impose on him even though he spoke to me first. I never did get a chance to ask him what he did for a living.

The basic difference, of course, is that religion is man's attempts to reach up to God. Christianity is about God reaching down to man in his love and man responding to that love. That act of God is explained in Philippians chapter two where it says of Jesus:

> Who, being in very nature God, did not consider equality with God something to be grasped, but made himself nothing, taking the very nature of a servant, being made in human likeness. And being found in appearance as a man, he humbled himself and became obedient to death—even death on a cross! Therefore God exalted him to the highest place and gave him the name that is above every name, that at the name of Jesus every knee would bow, in heaven and on earth and under the earth, and every tongue confess that Jesus Christ is Lord, to the glory of God the Father (Phil. 2:6–11).

We all are religious. Some deny it, but they do have a religion of their own making and will usually reveal what it is if given enough time to tell what they believe or don't believe. We all have faith, even if that faith is in ourselves. I sometimes get the feeling, while talking with others who are impressed with themselves, that it would take a radical conversion for that person to ever become part of a church worship experience. They are so enamored with their own minds, their own abilities, that they are the center of their own lives. To worship God would require that they could no longer worship themselves. These are often the same people who adamantly declare that they are not religious and are anti-faith. They have no idea that they demonstrate the opposite in their lives. It isn't faith or non-faith, it is faith and faith. The only difference between us is in who or what we worship.

When a person tells me that he is not religious, I may not argue with the comment by saying, "Yes, you are." But my antenna goes up as I listen for all the ways he shows that he is very religious. His religion just doesn't focus on God or on any of the formulated belief systems of the world. I know someone whose parents tried to make sure that she would not be religious (meaning Christian). Now she is practicing her own form of Hinduism. That doesn't surprise me. We will surrender to God or to something else but we will surrender even while thinking that we haven't surrendered to anything religious at all.

"Religion has caused so much trouble and pain in the world. We would be better off without any religion."

I agree that there has certainly been a lot of evil done in the name of religion. But I can also point to universities, hospitals, women's rights, child protection, all the work given to rebuilding devastated areas, and other good works that we see when church groups respond to emergencies and crises. That is mostly missing in places where there is no Christian influence.

When we see disasters, natural or manmade, it is notable that often the first responders are the Christians. The people in those places of suffering see it. Churches mobilize with caravans of help; Christian organizations are quickly on-site with people skills, medicines and food. If there is a "nonreligious" person serving there as well, he or she is more the exception than the rule. We are all the beneficiaries of the Christian people who have done great things—from the fight to eliminate slavery to the battle to help bring a cure for AIDs.

With the rise of militant Islamic movements, however, we see the dangers brought by religion. And when we hear hateful speech coming from militant-sounding "Christians," it seems to their hearers that we are all cut from the same cloth. But we aren't if we distinguish between those who bear in their lives the love of Christ as opposed to those who do not. To quote David Neff in a *Christianity Today* opinion piece, "We must learn to resist evil without demonizing or polarizing." If we do demonize or polarize, we are no different than any others. In that same article, Neff spoke of martyrs, people who have died for the faith and have not been combatants. He wrote, "The authentic martyr tradition emulates Jesus, who remained silent, '…like a sheep that before its shearers is dumb'" (Isa. 53:7, RSV).

We can point to the problems of religion but we can also point to the benefits brought to our world by people who are redeemed by Christ and are committed to serving Him. They are the ones who are also committed to serving others. No Christian believer has anything to apologize for when it comes to showing mercy and love even in the face of the religious evils going on around them, including those who claim that some of the evil people do is done in the name of Christ.

There is a lot of misinformation in our culture about true Christianity. It is lumped together with "religions." I can't argue with what is accurate or inaccurate about "religions," but I can do what Jesus called me to do, which is to love my neighbor as myself. If I do wrong, let me admit it. But my wrong can't be placed on Jesus. That's a message we just have to keep telling and showing so that our showing outshines our telling. And we have to admit that there are well-meaning but angry people who make strident, hateful statements while referring to themselves as Christians. They are particularly in our midst today in our divided nation.

For those of us who want to obey Jesus, on His terms, will we take advantage of where we are and the times we are living in to reach out to secular people with the message of the Savior? Will we bring to our world the Good News while there is still time?

chapter 7

While There Is Still Time

When I became a believer in the Savior, my family did not share my faith. In fact, they were strongly opposed to my Christian faith. I can remember my mother crying and saying to me, "We tried so hard to raise you well and now look what you have done."

It was more than two years later that the family also came to faith in Christ. And it happened because Christians were intentional. I remember when the turnaround came. My mother was suddenly taken ill in the night and was rushed to the hospital. Surgery was needed, and in the city of Detroit, where there were many doctors, the doctor called was also one of the advisors to the college-age group I had joined at church. He knew my parents' rejection of all that I believed.

In the middle of the night, climbing out of bed to go to the hospital, the doctor didn't know who his patient would be. He told me later that he did what he always did. He knelt by the bed and prayed for the patient who was waiting for surgery.

The surgery was successful, and by now the doctor knew who the patient was whom he had operated on. One day, during a post-operative visit, he said to my mother. "I want to tell you something. What your son has been telling you about Jesus is true. I am also a Christian."

There is much more to this story, but that was the turning point for my entire family. That surgeon was intentional, speaking to my mother about what was even more important than her physical condition. He cared about her soul. In his office that day he brought her to the Savior. In a very real sense he was used of God to save her life twice—once in the operating room and once forever. Soon after, one by one, the rest of my family came to saving faith in Christ.

Am I intentional about reaching out to those who need the Savior? Will God use me because I am in the way with Him?

A Lesson Learned

Intentionality is about being available for God to lead. When I was a university student and still a new Christian, I was part of a small group of InterVarsity Christian Fellowship students. One day one of the guys announced, "Tom came to Christ last night."

We all rejoiced at the news and then began to talk about our individual times with Tom. One by one the students said things like, "I was talking with Tom last week and this is what I said." Another replied, "I had been visiting with him the week before and this is what I said."

As we talked we began to see a pattern and realized that each one of us had said something to Tom about the Savior and each one, without knowing it, had built on the previous person's conversation with him. We had been orchestrated by the Holy Spirit to help Tom understand Jesus, each of us building on what the others had said without knowing that the others had even had their own conversations with him.

God knew what Tom needed and what each of us was to say in obedience to His leading. That's what the Holy Spirit does. A missionary friend once told me, "The Holy Spirit cannot germinate seeds we do not plant." We are to be in the way, intentional, willing to be used by God.

I never forgot that experience with Tom and it has influenced my own witnessing ever since. Who was the soul winner in that whole experience with Tom? It was none of us. It was the Holy Spirit. When I feel led to speak a word for Christ to someone, I never know who the Holy Spirit has used just prior to my speaking with that person. I can only be prayerfully intentional so that what I say follows what the Holy Spirit had that earlier witness say.

Placed in the Way of God

Caring about people who don't know the Savior is about deciding that I am going to place myself in the pathway of God and let Him guide me to the people who at this moment need the Savior and are ready for someone, like you and me, to help them come to saving faith.

King Jehoshaphat was told, "The battle is not yours…" (see 2 Chron. 20:15). That word spoken then is just as true for us now. Bringing people to the Savior is not ours to do. Our role is to be willing to be where God can do what God wants to do through us.

I have a great appreciation for the many believers where I live who have a burden for the lost. Many are intentionally praying and reaching out to others. I am grateful to God for each one. I hear how people are coming closer to the Lord because of the intentional witness of praying believers who really care. And they know the joy of seeing people come to Christ. I want more people to have that joy.

A Visit with John

One day, in Baltimore, Maryland, where I was working with the Billy Graham Crusade in that city, a woman called me. She told me that her 17-year-old son, John, was in Johns Hopkins Hospital where he was dying from cancer that was taking away his face. She was burdened because she didn't know whether or not her son was trusting in the Savior. She asked me to go see him.

I found him propped up in bed, much of his lower face disfigured. It was good that I had been told his age because the young man I saw could have been any age. He wore heavy-duty hearing aids because most of his hearing was gone. He could not speak because much of his lower jaw was destroyed by the cancer.

I stood directly in his line of sight and with careful expression of words so that he could read my lips as well as hear what he could through his hearing aids, I told him about his mother's concern for his soul. Then carefully, simply, I explained how John could receive Christ as his personal Savior.

If this was what he wanted, I asked him to raise his hand, thumb up. He did. I explained a bit more of what the Bible tells us about salvation so that I could be sure he understood. Again his thumb came up.

Then I told him I was going to pray, asking Jesus to come into John's heart, which I did. John was still focused on me, locked in. After my prayer I told him about eternal life and heaven and then said goodbye. As I started from the room, I turned and John's eyes were still following me and then his hand came up again, thumb up. That's what I told his mother.

The People around Us

Most of us work or live side-by-side with people who have missed out on the abundant life. Jesus said, "I have come that they may have life, and have it to the full" (John 10:10). There are people all around us who don't have that life. They are missing out on life now and could miss out on the life that is forever. They don't know it because they don't know that there is another life. We are the Good News bringers to help them see that there is another way.

One day, I was talking to a man who was 92 years old and in failing health. He had always been a faithful church member, yet he said he believed that there were many ways to God. Each person or each culture thinks their way is right, and who was he to say that there is only one correct way. All peoples have their versions of truth, so who can say which "truth" is correct.

For this man, Jesus was one option among many. Yet he had spent his entire life as a good church member. He didn't have any idea that Jesus is the way, the truth and the life. That was not his fault. There are many others like him all around us who have never heard the redemptive message of God.

I spent a lot of time with him before he died. I prayed for him as well. I do not know whether or not in the end he opened his heart to the Savior. I could only lay out the truth as simply as I knew how. I could not make him respond. But I had to be there—that is the believer's calling.

In his research, George Barna has found that a large proportion of people who are in our churches don't really know the basis of their faith. They haven't grasped the basic tenets of what Christianity is. These are the ones who either have not understood the Gospel or they may not have even heard the Gospel, having missed it during all their years in church. There are so many people around us like that who even if they heard the Good News may not have understood it.

I read about a man who was a good man, who grew up in church and realized much later in life that he was not a believing Christian. He came to faith after his children were grown. After all those years in church, not knowing about life and freedom and peace in Christ, here's what he said, "When a man is truly saved, God fills his heart with love and gives him a hunger for lost souls." He added, "The hunger He instilled within me is a hunger to witness to lost church members—the hardest people in the world to reach. I know there are thousands of people just like me who are mired in false traditions and security."

Am I willing to be like that man? Am I willing to engage nonbelievers in the community? Am I willing to speak with good church people who do not yet know the Savior? This man said they are among the hardest to reach. He was right.

Unwilling Christians

Not every Christian has a burden for lost people or is willing to go to them with the saving word of God. We hear things like, "That's what we pay the pastoral staff for." Or, "That's why we have the Alpha program." Or, "God can reach that person without my help." Or, if the person is old school and still believes what some of the older pastors taught, he may say, "Jesus died to save the world. Therefore the world is already saved. Our task is to help people live out what they already are."

Then there are those who were professional pastors or missionaries but, having entered retirement, they have lost all interest in reaching others for Christ. Apparently it was once a job; now the lost person no longer matters to them. As a professional they once seemed to have a burden for the lost. As retirees they no longer have that burden.

As a result of making excuses and not being available to the work of the Holy Spirit in redemption, two things happen. First, we live as unfaithful Christians; second, we miss out on the joy that God brings when He uses us to reach others with His Good News.

Some may argue that there is a gift of evangelism and they don't have it. That's partly true. It was said of Charles Finney that he could walk into a room and people fell to their knees in repentance. That doesn't happen when I walk into a room. Finney had a special God-given gift.

I heard a lot of Billy Graham's sermons over the 25 years that I worked and traveled with him. God gave him the gift of evangelism. I've seen that gift used just as effectively in one-on-one situations when Billy was talking to a single person about his need for the Savior as I did when he was preaching to packed stadium crowds.

In Seoul, South Korea, there were 1,100,000 people at one meeting in the great Yeoido Park. But I remember also when a Billy Graham Crusade was being held in Las Vegas, Nevada. Some people think there are no Christians in that city but there are, and they have a burden for the lost people who live and work around them. That's why they urged Billy Graham to come and hold meetings there.

The committee in charge of the event said that a lot of show people couldn't attend the evening meetings because they were working. Could something be held for them after they got off work? So one night, after the last show, about 2 a.m., we all met in a hotel hall where Billy gave a brief address and then walked around the room speaking to men and women individually.

I found myself standing next to a well-known singer who had been entertaining in one of the Las Vegas night spots. Billy Graham saw him, came over and without hesitation pointed to the man's heart, addressed him by name and asked, "How are things in there?" I quickly realized that I was standing on sacred ground and moved away so that Billy and the entertainer could speak privately. Whether addressing thousands or one person at a time, Billy Graham was always intentional.

But evangelism isn't so much about who has evangelistic gifts and who doesn't. It is about the obedience and availability of every believer.

My question to myself is not, "Am I willing to be a soul winner?" My question is "Am I willing to be where the Holy Spirit wants me to be as He brings men and women along the road that leads to the Savior?" Am I willing to be used by God to intentionally reach out to the people whom I know in my community or sphere of influence and help them to meet Jesus Christ as their personal Savior?

Ways of Our Own Choosing

A woman who had once described herself as an atheist said, "I sincerely believed that there was no God." But then she met God. Afterwards she said, "I had never considered myself a prisoner, but instantly I knew that I was free. I had never considered myself dead, but now I knew that I was alive."

Any of us could have told her that. But God had to show her. When we go intentionally to a person with the Good News, we know that God has already been at work in that person's life convicting and convincing because it is not God's desire that any should perish. Certainly Philip, as we read in the book of Acts, was in the right place at the right time to hear the Ethiopian reading Scripture. He was there to help the man understand what God was already showing that man.

The apostle Peter told us, "Salvation is found in no one else, for there is no other name under heaven given to mankind by which we must be saved" (Acts 4:12). Still, people will look for other ways to find God to suit their own preferences and their own choosing. Yet I've found that when I just say these words that Peter wrote and state why I believe what Peter said is true and explain how those words have worked themselves out in my life, people listen. I'm not angry or mean about it; I just believe it and explain it.

This and other passages from the Bible are wonderful Scriptures for me to point to when a person tells me that there are many ways to God. I just say, "Well, I come down on the side of what Jesus taught and what the Bible says about His teaching."

The Bible states, "He who has the Son has life..." (see 1 John 5:12). When a person challenges me about believing that biblical statement, I just admit it. "Yes, I do believe it," I tell him. I already know that deep down inside that individual is missing the life and meaning that Jesus offers. I know it because we were all made for God and I know that God is letting that person experience his own inner emptiness. I don't have to mention that emptiness; God is already showing him his emptiness.

People without God's redeeming wholeness don't know about life, they don't know about freedom, they don't know about peace. These are all gifts from God to those who have surrendered to Him. But people don't know, and often don't know anyone in their circle of friends who does know until a believing Christian intentionally comes into their lives.

That doesn't mean that we go to them in a forceful or obnoxious way. A person can't know what he doesn't know just because we say to him that he is missing wholeness and life. It is like trying to explain the ocean to a child who knows only the mud puddle he is playing in. That's his reality. He has no way of mentally expanding to something more until he is taken to the ocean and he sees it for himself.

But, unfortunately, there are well-meaning Christians whom I've met, who are keeping others from meeting the Savior because in their enthusiasm about winning others they think that bringing the light means shining a searchlight into that other person's eyes. That person will automatically shut his eyes and turn away. We may think that being salt means dumping it on or rubbing it into the wounds that so many people carry. Those Christians bring none of the benefits of light or salt; they bring only pain.

Intentional Where I Live

Am I intentional right where I live? Right where God has placed me? I may never know where God will use me. Just to say a word for Christ or to show the love of Christ may be all that is needed for someone to take the next step toward the Savior.

Here is an example told to me by a friend and classmate of many years ago. As a child, my friend lived in Germany during World War II. His father was drafted into the German army. His father wasn't a Nazi; he was just a citizen who got called up to serve. He was a conscript. But he had one specialty that most others didn't have. He spoke Russian. So he was placed as an officer over a Russian prisoner of war camp.

One evening, he felt he needed to go out and make one more sweep around the compound. As he walked, he saw a group of prisoners gathered near the fence listening to one of the men who was addressing the group. What was this? What were they planning? The German officer drew closer and listened.

The Russian prisoner was telling his comrades about how they could come to know Jesus as their personal Savior. My friend's father did what he knew he shouldn't have done without armed support. He unlocked the gate, went in and approached the group. They all pulled back in fear. Why was this German officer approaching them?

He stopped in front of the group and said, "What this man is telling you about Jesus Christ is true. I am also a Christian." And there in that prisoner of war camp a Russian prisoner and a German army officer fell into each other's arms and wept.

That Christian POW could have spent his time lamenting his capture, the situation he was in, the poor food. He could have complained that he was suffering. But he didn't. He was there and that place was his mission field. He was intentional.

That's what being intentional means. I can only imagine what the witness of those two sworn enemies embracing in a prison compound had on the other prisoners who were there. I suspect that none of those prisoners would ever forget that experience. And, they would have seen immediately that faith in Christ is much bigger than nationality or politics or even war. That is a good thing for every believer to keep in mind.

We are called to be "…always prepared to give an answer to everyone who asks you to give the reason for the hope that you have," explained the apostle Peter. Then he added, "Do this with gentleness and respect" (1 Pet. 3:15).

What Happens When We Intentionally Pray?

Prayer is the most important ministry that any of us can have. Everything else pales in the light of prayer. God answers prayer.

There are two types of praying. There is praying **for** someone and praying **with** someone. We tend to know more about the first than the second. So, I want to start with the second, which is praying **with** someone.

A friend told me that the biggest reason he has heard Christians give about not witnessing to others is, "I don't want to offend anyone." Well, I have found that prayer is not offensive to people unless the person who is praying is at the same time abrasive or obnoxious in his witness.

Anyone who has spent much time with people who do not know the Savior will realize that some people have gone through their entire lives without ever having had anyone pray with them. Most believers tend to take prayer as something we know very well. But there are people who have never had God's name and their name put together in the same sentence. These are the people who have always managed their own lives; they thought they didn't need God. They depended on themselves. It is not that they didn't have faith; it is that they had faith in themselves and only in themselves. They lived their lives with the god called "me."

One day I was sitting in a coffee shop in Halifax, Nova Scotia, where two women were talking at a nearby table. One said to the other, "I'm 50 years old now. If anything is going to happen in my life, I have to make it happen."

There are a lot of people who have lived their entire lives with that mantra, "I have to make it happen." But, toward the end of life, many of those self-sufficient people are discovering that they couldn't really manage their own lives. When their strength starts to fail, they find that all the ability they thought they once had to make things happen isn't working anymore. They have met the dead ends that they cannot surmount on their own. They find that they are different people as they age. Even Boomers, who tend to live in denial about aging, trying very hard not to acknowledge it even to themselves, have nowhere left to turn. Their god of self hasn't done for them what they thought their god would do.

Through prayer that person is being brought into the presence of God in an experience that he has never had before. I don't think most of us who pray often can imagine what that's like. We are so accustomed to having people pray with us and for us that it hasn't occurred to us that this is an experience many have never had.

When with a person and allowed to pray, I always pray for God's love to reach out to that person. We don't have to teach about God's love when we can pray for God's love to surround a person. Often I pray the very words that this individual has said about his inability to believe. If he said, "I can't believe that…," I'll weave that into my prayer. If he said, "I think the Bible is full of errors," I'll weave that into my prayer. If he said, "People who believe that Jesus is the only way are narrow," I will tell God that view in my praying with that person. His words spoken to me are woven into my prayer for him.

By my telling God what someone believes, that person realizes that God is listening to what he is saying and God knows what he believes. I don't lecture in prayer; I just vocalize what that person said about himself. That does several things. He knows that I have been listening to what he has been saying because I quoted what he said to me. Also, he knows that I am convinced that his statements of unbelief are important to God. He and his beliefs have been brought to the throne of the Father.

I am very bold in saying to God, "He believes that..." and finish the sentence with something that person says he believes or doesn't believe. I never add or subtract anything. By my words repeating his, that person is saying to God exactly what he had just said to me. I also thank God for that person's honesty, openness and willingness to listen. This opens up a natural avenue to God, something many people have never experienced before.

If during our conversation I had an opportunity to use a passage of Scripture to answer one of his questions, and I often do, I may bring that same passage of Scripture into my prayer, thanking God for the promise or statement that He gave to us and then repeating in my prayer what God said in Scripture. When I pray the Scripture that I had just used, that Scripture is always applied to what that person expressed about his situation or question of the moment.

Even With Only a Little Faith

Here's an example of praying with someone. The man I was with did not know what he believed. He saw so many different religions and figured that either they were all correct and right for each particular believer or none of them were true.

But I was given several opportunities to pray with him. And often I prayed what we had just discussed. I have no evidence that he came to faith, but as he was slipping away to death I knew that he had clearly been shown how we can be certain of eternal life.

Did he think about our conversations, or those prayers, or that Scripture in his moments alone before he died? I don't know. But he knew what he was invited to do: "Call on me and I will answer you" (see Jeremiah 33:3). That's a Scripture I could leave with him. I could also leave for his thinking, "You will seek me and find me when you seek me with all your heart. I will be found by you, declares the LORD" (Jer. 29:13). That's also a Scripture I could pray.

There are other words in Scripture that speak of coming to Christ, such as, "If you declare with your mouth, 'Jesus is Lord,' and believe in your heart that God raised him from the dead, you will be saved. For it is with your heart that you believe and are justified, and it is with your mouth that you profess your faith and are saved" (Rom. 10:9–10). If I had used those words in our conversation, I would usually repeat those same words in prayer.

I will often tell a person that I came to faith knowing that I couldn't just say words; I had to believe them in my heart. I couldn't just believe them in my heart, I also had to say the words. So our talk and the prayer always fit together.

The last words I was able to give to a man who was in hospice before he was no longer responsive was that he could tell God that even though he had all those uncertainties, he was still willing to reach out to the Savior. I always let a person know that he can exercise what little faith he has even if he still has questions or is uncertain about various matters. I certainly didn't know everything when I accepted the Savior. I had no biblical or theological understanding then. Whether a person does respond in his dying moments or does not, I may not know. But I can still open the door for him to see how he can give himself to Christ.

In praying with someone, I am able to express the saving message about Christ and ask God to help that person to receive the Savior. I am able to say, "Jesus said, 'Whoever comes to me I will never drive away'" (John 6:37). And then I will ask God to help this man reach out to Christ and to receive Him as Savior.

Here is my experience with another man I visited. At first, any attempt at saying anything about God was met with, "Well thank you for coming." I was dismissed. He was one of those self-sufficient, brilliant men who had had a distinguished academic career. But as he was in the hospital, the opportunities to pray with him started to come. Soon he welcomed prayer from me and from other Christians who visited him. In my praying, I asked God that if this man, and I called him by name, is reaching out to You now, inviting Jesus into his heart, please receive him and give him all that Jesus offers those who come to Him.

Why is that important? He is listening to someone speak to God on his behalf. And as I pray I add what he can do to open himself to the Savior. When that man slipped into a coma, I still prayed in his hearing, whether or not he could hear. Can a person give himself to God in a coma? I have no idea. But I can pray for him to do it.

We do not ever have to fear praying with a person who is antagonistic to the Gospel. Loving a person, and praying for him specifically, especially about a conversation that we just had will often open a closed heart.

Praying for Someone

When people are sick or facing a crisis, it is the best time to ask about praying **for** them. I will often tell a person that Andrea and I have a time of prayer together each evening. I tell them,

"We will pray for you in this situation." Because God is God and God is working, that is often the doorway to that person's soul.

Then we are not only praying for that person and the situation he is facing but we are also praying for that person's salvation. Later, I am able to remind that individual that we have been praying for him and will often ask, "How can we pray for you more specifically?" Some have never been prayed for by anyone else. This idea of being prayed for is something totally new to some people. Often, when that person tells me how he would like us to pray for him about a specific need or situation, I'll promise him that we will pray and then add, "Let me pray for you right now. May I?" Just about every person will say yes.

When we pray for someone, we open the door to a person even when we are saying nothing directly to that person. That person could be across town or across the country. God is working, preparing and seeking that person. The Holy Spirit knows no limits. We can trust that God is answering our prayer and we can be certain that something is happening in that other person's mind and heart. Prayer is the greatest work we can have when bringing God and that person together.

Many of the people whom I meet in one capacity or another are prayed for. The people I pass on the street are prayed for. Even people who are in the church I attend are prayed for. I am still surprised by how God will open doors to give an opportunity for a word about the Savior or the chance to pray with that person personally, even when I wasn't expecting it.

When I was a university student and a new Christian, I prayed for my unsaved family; others did too. But lacking experience with prayer, I didn't think my family could ever come to Christ. I came to think that some people were too hardened and beyond God's reach. Then a friend gave me a verse of Scripture to cling to: "Though we believe not, yet he abideth faithful. He cannot deny himself" (2 Tim. 2:13, KJV). Or, as this verse is presented in a more modern version, "If we are faithless, he will remain faithful, for he cannot disown himself."

I realized that other people were intentionally praying for my family. I was not alone in my praying. God was working in their lives as others were praying for them. God was faithful even when I could not believe that He could work in my family.

A Life behind the Praying

When we pray with or for someone, we had better have a life that backs up what we are saying. Here's an example of what I think intentional prayer is not. I know a man who says he is trusting in Jesus as his Savior. He boldly tells an unbelieving friend of ours that he is praying for her. But he tends to run roughshod over people; he curses regularly. She politely tells him, "Well, a lot of people are praying for me," and then brushes him off.

I would rather just pray for that person quietly, apart from her, than to tell her that I am praying for her and then not back up what I am saying with my life. This woman doesn't know that Andrea and I are praying for her. At this point we have a warm relationship with her and we want that to continue.

Here is another example of what I think intentional prayer is not. A retired pastor boasted that he had seen 43 people at Walmart and 50 people at Home Depot pray the "sinners' prayer," all within the brief time he was there.

He had printed up a prayer card and walked through the stores handing out the prayer cards to the people he passed. He didn't stop to talk to any of the people; he didn't listen to them to find out where they were in their spiritual journey. He just distributed his cards. When he saw people reading the card, he said they were praying that prayer. But were they? If we don't come alongside a person, love that person, build a relationship with that person and know how to pray specifically for that person, we may not only miss opportunities ourselves but we may inoculate that person against hearing real prayer and a real witness.

When I speak of intentional praying, I'm not talking about throwing out general, one-size-fits-all prayer cards at people. That can actually prevent people from serious considerations of the Savior. I am talking about carefully praying for people by name.

Will I always see the answers to my prayers? No, nor does God owe me that information. We are called to pray; we aren't promised that we will see the answers. It is enough that the Bible tells us, "The prayer of a righteous person is powerful and effective" (James 5:16). That's all we need to know.

The Story of Mary

This next true story may not seem like a prayer story, but stay with it.

When I read James 5:16, "The prayer of a righteous person is powerful and effective," I think of Mary.

When I read that great faith chapter, Hebrews 11, and look at verse 13 that tells me, "These all died in faith without having received the promises," I think of Mary.

Do I really believe that my prayers are powerful? Can I go for years believing those words in Scripture while God seems so silent? Will I still believe even if God may not answer my prayers during my lifetime? I think of Mary.

Mary grew up in Detroit, Michigan, in the 1890s. As a young teen she was sent to live in a place called "The Home for Bad Girls." People didn't have fancy names for places like that back then; they just called it what it was.

Did Mary have a praying mother and father? Did they agonize over their daughter? Nobody knows. Mary was not a Christian.

At age 17 or 18, Mary was sent to work as a cook on a farm in Lenawee County, Michigan. She cooked for the family and the farm hands.

Charles, one of the farmer's sons, fell in love with Mary, and they wanted to get married. But, at first, Charles's father wouldn't allow it because Charles was a few months shy of 21 and in those days a boy had to work for his father until he was 21 or pay for the months of lost labor.

Charles and Mary got married, moved to an uncle's farm to work, and Charles paid off his father from his wages, an amount agreed upon based on the value of the lost labor that Charles would have given his dad. Years went by and Charles was able to borrow enough money to buy a farm of his own. Neither Charles nor Mary was a Christian.

Soon children came along. Nine children were born; one died in infancy, leaving a family of eight children. The children were raised on the farm where they had neither church nor Christian teaching. None of them were Christians.

During the depths of the Great Depression in the 1930s, unable to keep up with his mortgage or the taxes, Charles lost his farm. They moved to town where Charles got a job in a factory. By then most of the children were grown and on their own. None were Christians.

Somehow, in some way and for some reason, Mary began to attend a church in that town and bought a Bible. On a table by her chair, the Bible was always at hand with her reading glasses marking the place where she last read. That's when Mary became a Christian. Had her mother been praying for her all those years? Did she know that Mary was now a believer? Nobody knows.

Now that Mary had given her heart and life to Christ, she began praying for her children; she prayed for her grandchildren too. None of them were Christians.

Mary died from a massive stroke at age 60. Her prayers for her children and grandchildren had not been answered. Like the faithful men and women told about in Hebrews 11, she died in faith, believing. She never received the promise. No one in her family was a Christian.

Even on the day of her funeral, it was clear that the family was rather calloused. Mary's funeral was conducted by her minister, a preacher who waved his arms, stomped around and shouted a lot. For the adults it was entertainment; for the children it was both fascinating and frightening.

Later, back at the house following Mary's burial, the women went into the kitchen to prepare a meal while Charles pulled out a deck of cards, got the men together, and soon they had a poker game going with lots of joking and laughing. One of Charles's daughters came out of the kitchen, saw what the men were doing and lit into her dad, reminding him that his wife was less than an hour in the ground. He didn't see the problem but, shrugging his shoulders, put the cards away to avoid further nagging.

More years went by. Then, one by one, at different times, in different places and under various circumstances, Mary's children and grandchildren began to come to faith in Christ—all but one daughter who died before age 40 of alcoholism.

As Mary's children and grandchildren came to accept the Savior, in some cases the children became Christians first and the parents followed; in other families it was the parents who first believed. The numbers of Christians kept expanding. Cousins who lived in different cities and different states began comparing notes and were surprised to learn that this cousin, and that one, was now a Christian. The man who had once been known as a wild kid was now a follower of Jesus. The person who used to drink heavily was now sober and a Christian. The redeeming work of Christ was spreading everywhere among them.

By the time great grandchildren and then great-great grandchildren came along, the number of Christian families was extensive; men and women and young people were coming to faith in ever-increasing numbers, serving the Lord, active in their churches; some were in ministry.

So many of Mary's family are Christians today it would be hard to add up the numbers. Yet Mary had not lived to see any of it. She clung to the promises and died in faith, believing.

For any who, right now, are praying for a son or daughter who is not yet in the kingdom, I urge them to think of Mary. To the people burdened for a grandchild who is not walking with the Lord, I say, "Think of Mary."

Might it be that God will answer our prayers for those lost family members after we are gone? Are we willing to trust God that, "The prayer of a righteous person is powerful and effective," even if we never live to see it? Can we rest in the truth of Hebrews 11 and, like those saints of old, die in faith, believing? Think of Mary.

Mary was my grandmother.

God will honor our commitment to pray. Whether we see answers in our lifetime or we don't, isn't what is important, God will honor our faithfulness as we intentionally pray for others. John 6:44 tells us, "No one can come to me unless the Father who sent me draws him." So I am praying that the Father will draw them. That's intentional praying.

While There Is Still Time...

As long as God allows us life and strength to help others meet the Redeemer, we are called to take hold of every day and prayerfully come alongside others who do not yet know the peace that passes understanding or the assurance of sins forgiven. While there is still time, we are to continue faithfully praying.

When Billy Graham turned 95 years old and was no longer the vibrant person he was in earlier years, he still had a burden for those without the Savior. He had a nationwide outreach called "My Hope America" in which Christians from more than 28,000 churches invited others into their homes to watch and discuss the telecast or a video that included comments by Billy Graham about redemption and the cross. Even so late in life, for Billy Graham there was still time.

We have friends, former students of ours, who, after full lives and professional careers, are now missionaries in their retirement years in what we call a closed or limited-access country. They tell us about their language study. Why do they want to learn the language of the people where they now live? They are learning the language so that they can hear what is said by others, understand what others are saying and then speak to them by replying to what they have heard and understood. They hear, understand and reply. They make this effort because for them even in the latter years of their productive lives there is still time.

We are missionaries, too, right where we live, while there is still time.

The Danger of an Agenda

What about witnessing "plans" and "steps"? Some Christians don't witness to the saving work of Jesus; they are dispensing machines. Push a button and words about Jesus come out. We need to be aware that most people around us have heard our Christian "pitch" before. They know the words. They can see them coming. They can tell when we are trying to steer a conversation. Then they will feel manipulated, treated more as an object than a person.

We can look at plans and steps from two different directions: Plans are good if they are part of our thinking. Plans are not good if used only as formulas.

It doesn't help if we only have an agenda, a next step in the plan to read to someone. When we do that, we already know what we are going to say. We aren't listening. We talk, put a comma in place and wait while that person speaks, and then we go back to the presentation of our plan.

I cannot reach out to a neighbor whom I refuse to understand and I can't understand him if I refuse to listen when he speaks. I can't simply throw words out at him from behind my wall. If I build a wall between us, I may feel safe, even comfortable behind my wall, but if I am hiding behind my wall, I can't put my arm around that other person's shoulder.

If other Christians are behind that wall with me and we speak only to each other about those who are on the other side of our wall, and compare notes and agree that we know the thinking of those on the other side of the wall and only toss words over the wall that answer what we have decided among ourselves that the other person is saying or asking, we are not being faithful to the loving Christ.

It is good for me to have a plan in mind so that I know where I am going. But I control the plan; the plan doesn't control me. I know that an unsaved person has to come to the place of surrender to the Savior. I know that he has to understand sin and its consequences. I know that he will then need assurance of salvation based on God's Word. But that plan in my mind is to help me have hooks, pegs upon which to place the Scriptures in my mind that will help that person. It isn't a rote formula for me to simply regurgitate.

We Are Greeks

Most of us are Greeks in our thinking. We are logical. We see a plan of salvation and it makes perfect sense to us. For us A+B=C. But does it make sense to the other person who may be more Hebrew in his thinking? He may be more into story and feeling, not our logic.

Add to that the Internet way of informing that gives us pieces—a bit of this, a bit of that, and we put it all together in a way that suits us. We will know how to approach a person with God's message only if we understand his thinking process, whether he is more Hebrew or Greek.

When I started writing articles for *Decision* magazine, I could write one long article containing all of the information that was needed. By the time I left *Decision* 25 years later, I was writing the same content but presenting it in small chunks or pieces. The readers could not handle long sections of gray copy. They needed subheads for eye breaks, decks, sidebars with different colors in the background—anything to break up the copy so that the person could read this little piece or that little piece as he chose. The same content was there, but no longer in one complete story.

If we are talking with older people, we are still dealing mostly with Greeks. Our words—presented as a logical plan—may communicate well. But that doesn't mean we can just dispense our rules or steps or laws logically to a younger person who bases his learning on a fact here, another there, glued together into a whole that he has put together in his own way in his own mind.

And, of course, the teaching of the relativistic world has influenced every age group. In his book *Evangelism OUTSIDE THE BOX*, Rick Richardson writes, "Any attempt to claim that one has the truth for everybody is experienced as an arrogant, offensive attempt at domination and control." He goes on to say, "People are crying out not so much for philosophical answers as for a way to give meaning and purpose to personal and corporate pain and suffering."

We may understand our logical plan of salvation where we are coming from. But that other person may be coming from a different direction. We know our Christian story; it makes sense to us. The other person has probably heard some parts of the Christian story as well, but has selected what is true for him if he selects any part of it at all.

If we charge in blindly with our biblical message and assume that the other person is coming from the same perspective that we have ourselves, and that he understands what we understand the way that we do, we could go right past that person. In my teaching of writers, I have to remind them that as the author they know everything; the reader knows nothing. Don't make the reader guess about your meaning. If he does, he could guess wrong and become confused. Then it is hard to get him back into the story. The same is true in our verbal presentation of the Gospel. If we confuse our hearers with our presentation, they may simply stop listening. Many have stopped listening to the Christians around them.

Foundations Aren't the Whole House

There are evangelism plans out there that are good as foundations but not as ends in themselves. If I know the "Roman Road," the "Four Spiritual Laws" or "Steps to Peace with God," that's for me to know. It is foundational to give me a basis for explaining the way to new life in Christ.

It is possible, when we are only formulaic, that a person might agree with what we are saying, and then we assume that because he has agreed with the formula or the plan he has therefore agreed with Jesus. These plans are good as a foundation and even as framework. But if all we do is read the plan to someone, we may only have brought him to agree with the plan—not the Savior. He may accept my formula but still not meet the Living Christ. I'm always leery of the boastful Christian who gets on a plane in Detroit and by the time he lands in Chicago has led everyone around him on the plane to pray the prayer of salvation.

There are a lot of inoculated people who have accepted a plan, agreed with a series of steps, agreed with a formula, but haven't really had a personal encounter with Christ. Worse, because they did what we asked them to do, they feel they are "done."

Following rules, a plan or church catechism can give the person the sense that he has made it. He is safe. But he may not be. He has simply done the steps, the plan, so he can become quite unreachable to another Christian who wants to explain to him what it really means to become a follower of Jesus.

We need to realize that when we talk to each other, as believers, we understand where we are coming from. That's because we who are believers have the same frame of reference. But when we talk to an unbeliever, his frame of reference is probably not the same as ours. We make a mistake if we think that all we have to do is overpower him with our logic.

The Danger of Evangelistic Consumerism

Another problem we face with a person who has responded to a formula or a plan is that we have made it so easy for that person to agree with our plan or formula that it becomes all about the person himself and what he did, not about the Savior and what He did.

That's the danger of consumerism. The Christian has a product to sell; the consumer or unbeliever has bought the product. Then it is no different than buying a new vacuum cleaner or a computer. "Look at the computer I bought? This is my computer. *I* accepted Jesus as *my* Savior. I did it."

We have stressed "you and Jesus." You are the **consumer.** You invite him, the **product**, into your heart. So it is all about what **you do** to get saved. We have let the person believe that salvation is based on consumer gratification. Being a Christian becomes what I did to be saved and what salvation does for me, not about Jesus and what He did to save us. Self-reliance, even when I am relying on what *I* do with Jesus, is still all about me and I may never meet the life-changing Christ.

Scripture teaches, "By grace are you saved through faith, and that—**this faith gift of grace**—is not of yourselves. It is the gift of God." Is that person coming as a recipient of a gift that he cannot earn? We want people to step into the way of the Gift that God is offering in Christ Jesus (see Ephesians 2:8–9).

Our Christian Jargon

I've taught several times at a particular theological seminary in the south helping doctor of ministry students learn how they can expand their ministry through writing. I'd see papers written by a student who wrote of someone, "He went forward."

I'd ask the student "What does that mean?"

He'd reply, "Well, you know, he was accepting Christ."

"Oh, had he rejected Christ?" By that time the student was becoming frustrated with me. Maybe that person he was writing about was coming to faith or maybe that person was only following a cultural activity and hadn't met the Savior at all.

Or, there might be a time in a Sunday school class when the teacher asks 12-year-olds, "How many here want to become Christians and be baptized?" Usually every hand will go up. What child wants to be left out? But were they followers of church custom and culture or were they believers in Jesus?

One recent spring I was judging evangelism articles for the Evangelical Press Association. The magazine articles were submitted for awards. What I often found were a lot of programs about evangelism that the church could do, but all those programs really taught was how the church members could follow the program—do the steps. So for many, talking with a person about the Savior is not based on where that other person is or what he already believes; evangelism is only about doing the steps.

If I use certain words, will those words help or hurt? Years ago, as a student chaplain, I was doing my clinical work at a state psychiatric hospital. A classmate innocently told one of the patients that God was her Heavenly Father. That night she hung herself. Her concept of "father" was so painful that the thought of God being a father was too much for her. There was nothing wrong with what that student chaplain said. The problem was that he didn't know what those words meant to the other person. He hadn't listened.

When we listen to a person, we will move away from church jargon, clichés, plans or programs as something to dispense and enter as much as we can into that other person's life and experience.

Becoming Friends

In some cases we think evangelism, communicating the Good News of the Savior, is simply being friends with an unsaved person. Well, of course, we have no connection with a person if we are not friends, but is the act of simply offering friendship all we do? For example, a Christian who was practicing friendship evangelism told me that he met an unsaved friend in a bar rather than going home to what he really wanted to do that evening, which was to be with his family. But, bottom line, the unsaved friend knew only that this guy was friendly. Nothing was exchanged between them about the Savior.

No one responds to an unfriendly person. Surely we want to be friends and build bridges. But friendship with an unbeliever doesn't save. Only Jesus saves. We don't talk *at* people with a plan or program. We talk *to* people about Jesus who is the way, the truth and the life.

Remember That the Holy Spirit Is the Soul Winner

How can I help a person place his faith in Jesus? I am not the winner of souls; the Holy Spirit is. We can do harm for the Gospel when we push in and assume that conversion is our job. When we are trusting in the work of the Holy Spirit, we don't drive hard as though the saving of that person's soul is all up to us. It may be better to be still and know that He is God. As one Christian said, "We do a terrible job at trying to be the Holy Spirit."

Start where the person is; help that person where she is. There is no one way to be a soul-winning person. As we are intentional and in tune with the Holy Spirit, and if we are listening so that we hear the person we are talking to, God will use us in different ways with different people. There is no set pattern to soul winning.

An Owl in the Desert

Ruth Graham was in England where her husband, Billy, was holding evangelistic meetings. One day she went into Foyles Bookshop. The clerk was a sad looking man, dejected, and so Ruth struck up a brief conversation with him. She couldn't talk to him about the Lord right there in the store where he was waiting on customers, so she handed him an invitation to the evangelistic meeting that night.

The following year Ruth was back and again went to Foyles. That same clerk was there, only now he was smiling and full of energy. She asked, "What happened to you?" He replied, "Last year you were here and gave me an invitation to your husband's meetings. I went and met the Savior. He has changed my life."

As they talked a bit longer, Ruth asked, "Tell me what text my husband was preaching about that night?"

"Oh," he said, "I'll never forget it. He was preaching on Psalm 102:6, 'I am like a pelican of the wilderness: I am like an owl of the desert'" (KJV).

Now to me that is not an evangelistic text. But it hit that man right where he was. He explained, "A pelican shouldn't be in the wilderness. That's not where he belongs. Owls can't thrive in the desert. They are not at home there." It was what that man needed to hear, and the Holy Spirit knew it.

Agreeing with God

When a person we are witnessing to understands and is open and honest and sees his need, it is the next step for us to help him place his faith in the Savior. We can't assume he knows how to do that. I didn't know before I was a believer. I needed others to help me along the way.

As we pay attention to the person and pay attention to the Holy Spirit, we will know what is needed to bring that person to a decision. There are some basics:

1. He has to agree with God regarding the separation between himself and God caused by sin. God is Holy. That has to be understood. But remember that a person might not understand that word sin. We might be talking right past each other. "Sin" is missing the mark.

For many people, sin is what we do. But in God's word, we see that sin is what we are. What we do comes out of what we are. Even if, somehow, we never acted out a sin, we would still be sinners. We are separated from the holiness and righteousness of God. We have to work through with that person what it is we are talking about when we use the word "sin." We can't assume that the word has any meaning to a person. This could take time. The 15-minute race through a formulaic presentation probably won't work if we leave the person confused about what we are talking about.

Sin means going away from God. Conversion is turning around and moving back toward God. In sin, we are in opposition to God. We have been saying "No" to God. Now we are deciding to say "Yes" to God.

We don't set the standard by which God will accept us. God has set that standard and God, by His grace, has provided the answer, the solution, the way back.

So it is not a matter of, "I don't feel that I am a sinner." It isn't a matter of our own feelings at all; it is a condition. It is a state that we are in. In Romans 3:23 the apostle Paul explains this well, "For all have sinned and fall short of the glory of God." And "There is no one righteous, not even one" (Rom. 3:10). We can read on in that passage if it will help the person to understand what sin is and what it does to us.

I always make sure that we are on the same page, talking about the same thing. It will probably mean taking the time to draw that other person out as to his own understanding of what it means to be separated from God by sin. I turn to Scripture that will help the most with the person I am talking to. I always carry a New Testament with me when I call on people. It's in my pocket so it is easy to pull out. There is a separation between people and God, and we will talk about that as long as that person needs to.

2. He has to agree with God about who Jesus is and why He died and rose again. This too can create a problem. Who is Jesus today

besides a swear word? What does He have to do with me? The person might say, "I thought we were talking about God. Why is Jesus suddenly the topic?" There is a woman I know who is just beginning to connect in her mind that Jesus has something to do with Christianity. It had never occurred to her before. She didn't come to that quickly; it was a long process for her. We may even need to explain the birth and ministry of Jesus because that other person may not know.

3. I have to be sure to bring in the crucifixion and why it was needed and to bring in the resurrection too. I remember being with Billy Graham in Russia when he asked the Patriarch of the Russian Orthodox Church if he had any suggestions for Billy about his sermons. The Patriarch replied, "Yes, spend more time talking about the resurrection."

He had a good point. As important as it is to understand the reason for the crucifixion, it is equally important to clarify the importance of the resurrection. Jesus died, but He isn't dead. The risen Christ is the saving Christ. He died for our sins and rose again, overcoming and defeating death. The life He now offers is a post-grave life. It is everlasting life.

All of this may take a lot of time to work through. We may know our Christian history, how Jesus came, why He came, what He did for us and why. But we can't assume that the person we are speaking to understands. Don't move on if he is in a fog.

4. A person has to express to God his desire to place his faith in God's Saving Son. The Bible tells us, "If you declare with your mouth, 'Jesus is Lord,' and believe in your heart that God raised him from the dead, you will be saved. For it is with your heart that you believe and are justified, and it is with your mouth that you profess your faith and are saved" (Rom. 10:9–10).

I will often ask, "Is there any reason why you can't place your trust in Christ right now?" Or I might ask, "Is there anything preventing you from receiving the Savior right now?" If there is, that is the time to deal with it. There is no point in going further if the person still has questions. Deal with his questions and then come back to the question about receiving Christ.

I will sometimes use John 3:16 because he probably knows it or has heard it, especially if he is an older person. And, often, I will put his name into that verse.

When I sense that this person is ready, I explain that I will pray, telling God what this man is doing. Then I want him to pray and, in his own words, tell God what he is doing. It is his voicing of his own desire to have the Savior that will cement it for him.

5. Afterwards, a person will need scriptural assurance that peace with God is his. If I am already in the book of Romans, I will stay there and show him, "Therefore, since we have been justified through faith, we have peace with God through our Lord Jesus Christ, through whom we have gained access by faith into this grace in which we now stand. And we boast in the hope of the glory of God" (Rom.5:1–2). Or, "Therefore, there is now no condemnation for those who are in Christ Jesus" (Rom. 8:1). I want to make sure that his assurance isn't coming from me but from God. I don't want to be a packaged Christian; I want to be an honest, helpful Christian.

There is another step that is so often ignored. We who put our trust in Christ obey Him, follow Him and serve Him in the church. We are part of His body of believers. That church connection is as much a part of salvation as is the delivery of a baby into a family at birth. A baby isn't on his own the moment he is born. He is in need of nurture and care in every respect. That's what the church does. It serves as a pediatric ward.

There is a protection, a covering that is part of being within or under the care of the church. When people drift away from fellowship with other believers, somehow thinking that being a

Christian is personal and therefore has nothing to do with other believers, they soon go cold and end up as easy prey for Satan. So we stress the need to be a part of a Bible-believing church.

In our desire to help someone become a follower of Jesus, God will use what we know. Yes, be a Bible learner, become equipped, but God will use what we know now. Jesus said that we are not to worry about what we want to say or how we say it (see Matt. 10:19–20). That's because we are consciously, intentionally, relying on God for our replies and statements when speaking with another person about his soul. We have no other agenda except that the person we are speaking to comes to understand who the Savior is and how to know the Savior. When we are intentional about it, God can use us. Don't let your limited knowledge hold you back from helping a person come to faith.

Being a Person of Peace

It was said of Jesus, "He has done everything well" (Mark 7:37). I think that's what each of us would like people to say of us as followers of Jesus.

Jesus brings peace to troubled souls. When a person is alone, away from the crowd and all the other things that a person engages in to help him forget his unsettled soul, he is often quite honest about lacking peace. That's because there is only one Person who brings that needed peace. He is the Prince of Peace. I want to be a person of peace who brings the message of peace to others. I don't want people to miss out on Jesus because of me. I want to do no harm. We are called to be people of light. Jesus made that very clear to everyone who claims to belong to Him.

chapter 8

Letting the Light Shine

Years ago, while living on the East Coast, I read a newspaper article about a Christian who was "letting his light shine." He erected on the roof of his house a large neon sign that flashed the words "Jesus Saves." All night long the sign was flashing on and off. The neighbors complained and the man let it be known that he was being persecuted for righteousness sake.

Yet that man had part of his plan right. We are light and we are to let our light shine. Jesus said so.

If Jesus is the light of the world—and He is, and if He calls believers to "so shine your light among men"— and He does, then that is what we are supposed to do. He warned us against hiding that light under a basket rather than placing it high on a lampstand so that all may see by it.

But when we have taken the light and done with it the exact opposite of what Jesus told us to do, and have put our light under a bowl or basked, we have no excuse or complaint when the people around us continue to stumble around in the dark. Dark is dark because there is an absence of light. If our world seems to be getting darker, why are we complaining? Why have we hidden the light? In the dark, people can't see. In the dark, there is no way to know that there is any other way to live. When the light is uncovered, the darker the night, the brighter the light will appear and will draw people to it. But too often I see

Christians covering the light. As a result, all that others can see is the basket. Here's an example of what I mean.

Vocal Christians

All around us we are hearing loud, vocal Christians, some with a platform that draws the attention of the media, declaring non-light issues as central to the Christian faith. They don't have much contact with the average man on the street; they live removed even sheltered lives. But they are voices, usually strident voices, that repeat slogans, Christian jargon, and usually regurgitate the same verses of Scripture regardless of the questions they are asked.

These vocal Christians do not bring light; they disguise it or hide it. They don't speak for the average thinking Christian. Often they are an embarrassment to the thinking Christian. But they draw the attention of the media and the culture as a whole. They think they are defending the faith, but rarely is it faith in Christ that they are defending. It is their own views about what is wrong with society or the political structures. Other Christians may think that these vocal Christians are defending the faith, but that's because these vocal Christians have a few key words that make them sound like they are hitting important notes of biblical Christianity. To unbelievers, however, these vocal Christians communicate something other than the Good News of Jesus. To unbelievers, these vocal Christians sound like militant Muslims. Whether someone is defending the Koran or the Bible, to an unbeliever it all sounds like the same hateful speech. In a dark world, these who hide the Gospel under their social or political bushel basket don't bring light; they cause more darkness.

The Light Still Shines

But when I read about faithful Christians, especially young people who are committed to missions, I realize that the light still shines. When I read about young believers who are transforming evangelicalism from within, I find that they are comfortable with secular minds and uncomfortable with the political captivity of the Christian faith. When I hear about the dedication of those who pledge their lives to Christ at an InterVarsity Urbana conference or a Leo Giglio conference, I can see that the light still shines. When I go elsewhere in the world and see what God is doing through dedicated believers there, I know that the light still shines.

Not long ago I was teaching in Kyrgyzstan. Those I was teaching were evangelical Christians with a burden to reach their country with the Good News of Christ. In attendance there were newspaper editors, fiction writers, publishers and poets. There were even song writers. They were focused not on peripheral things but on the main thing—announcing the biblical faith. It isn't always easy for them (they have to live within certain governmental limits), but they are using the freedom they have. When I asked if there was a country that impressed them the most about the faithful Christians who lived there, they said with one voice, "South Korea."

While some Christians in my own country have chosen to hide the light of the Gospel under their political or social baskets, many in other countries have not. I've read about refugees from Iraq who are coming to faith in Christ in what was once known as East Germany. I hear about missionaries from other countries being sent to other parts of the world by their churches. I've met some of them too.

When I was teaching at the Reformed Theological College in Kampala, Uganda, a school that was reaching young men and women who were preparing for ministry in Uganda and other neighboring African countries, I was impressed by who was teaching, directing and financing the school. They were Koreans sent by churches in South Korea, with all the costs of the college paid for by Korean Christians.

We don't always see what God is doing elsewhere. Believers in the United States can get involved in so much that isn't central to the mission and work of Christ that we assume others in the world are doing the same. In most cases, they aren't. The church may not be vibrant and growing in the United States and other Western countries, but look at what is happening in Asia, Latin America or Africa; it is a different story. Even in places where life is hard and persecution is real, the light shines. In many developing parts of the world the Christian church is expanding exponentially. It is a story that needs to be told, although perhaps it is already so expansive that no one can put his arms around it to put that story into words. God cannot be limited or contained in our own little corner of the evangelical world.

God has His people everywhere; they are committed, worshipful and faithful. I remember talking with a woman in Moscow. She told me through an interpreter, "I always knew that the priest could talk to God in the cathedral. But now that I have Jesus, I have a cathedral in my heart." I've watched over the years as an increasing number of Bible-believing evangelical Christians in Russia have been getting a sound theological education, are starting churches and are seeing a spread of the message of Christ. It is happening in many places.

One day, when Andrea and I were in South Africa, we were driving back to our hotel in Cape Town after a pleasant trip down to where the Atlantic and the Indian oceans meet. There was a market along the road, women selling hand-crafted objects spread out on blankets. We stopped to look. As we moved along, looking at all of the hand-made goods and thinking about what we might purchase, I said to Andrea, "That woman back there is a Christian, I think." How did I conclude that when we had only talked with her about her products? Well, there really is a connection where my spirit bears witness with another's spirit that we are the children of God. So we went back to that woman, made our purchase, and then I said, "You're a Christian aren't you?" Her face lit up and pointing to her heart she said, "Jesus lives here."

General Secretary of the Egyptian Bible Society, Ramez Attala, tells how in spite of persecution and church burnings, the Christians in Egypt are growing in number and deepening in their all-out commitment to Christ. He says, "Live the Gospel and the world will pay attention."

The Light Will Be Seen. We Can't Miss It.

I've had the privilege of attending all three International Conferences for Itinerant Evangelists where thousands of Christians from around the world met together in Amsterdam, the Netherlands. When there were times of prayer for our various nations, I saw people praying in their own way, in their own language, many even prostrate on the floor. Afterwards, the floor was wet from the tears of these praying Christians who wanted so much for their own people to know the Savior. The light shines!

Because I reported what I saw God doing at so many of Billy Graham's evangelistic meetings over the years, I met a lot of people who were bringing light and many who were receiving the light. One evening, in a stadium of a large city, I decided to move away from the press table and go way up into the top bleachers because I knew that was usually where a lot of teenagers gathered. They were there, laughing and having fun until the sermon. When Billy Graham stood to preach, a hush came over those teens. And when the invitation was given urging men and women and young people to give their hearts to Christ, I stood up with my back to the top wall so that I could see what was happening.

I watched as one by one many of those teens stood to their feet and made their way forward. It wasn't a group response; rather, it was all individuals, one after another. It was a deeply moving sight. Then, glancing to my right I noticed that I was standing next to a police officer who was watching the same scene unfold. As I became aware of him, I noticed that he had removed his cap and that tears were rolling down his cheeks. Here was a man who knew street crime and gangs. He also knew what he was seeing. The light was shining there, in that place, on that night.

Don't Let the Light Go Out

When the light is uncovered, when the basket is taken away, when the light is up on a lampstand where it can send its beams everywhere, people see the One who said, "I am the light of the world."

How do we unwrap Jesus from what has been put on Him socially, culturally and politically? How can we reach people who have heard things about the Christian faith that are different from the story of the Son of God that the Father wants them to hear? How do we reach the unsaved who think they already know what Christianity is? How do we explain the light when all some people have seen is the basket that so many Christians have put over that light?

I find myself wondering how I can get past all of the clutter that has been heaped on the Gospel so that I can point people to the Savior. What do I need to do in order to undo what other Christians have done when they have replaced Jesus with something else?

I find myself looking at my fellow believers from the perspective of those who don't know Jesus. If I go to a person to talk about the Savior, what is he really hearing? Does he know that I am a follower of the God of love? Does he know that I am a person who is trying to obey the Prince of Peace? Does he know that I am an ambassador with a message of redemption and heaven? Or does he assume that I am an angry person who wants to tell other people how they ought to live?

How do I approach the unsaved person who has seen only the cultural, political basket and not the light of Christ? I can point to God's majesty. I can point to the message that is based not on invented stories but on what a follower of Jesus has experienced. I can try to move my hearers from a cluttered gospel to what happens when the uncluttered message of Jesus is clearly presented. I can point to what happens when even one individual meets the Savior.

Here is an example of what I mean about just one person coming to saving faith. It is the story of Tommy Bewes whose grandson, Richard Bewes, followed John Stott as rector of All Souls, Langham Place in London.

A maid working in the Bewes household asked her employer if on her night off she could go hear the evangelist D. L. Moody who was in London. And she asked if she could take young Tommy with her? Permission was granted.

That night, under the preaching about the saving work of Jesus, little Tommy Bewes gave his heart to Christ. Many years later, when Tommy was then an old man, his grandson, Richard, said that his grandfather told him that he had been making a list and had found that more than 100 members of their extended family were in Christian ministry. They were missionaries, pastors, Scripture Union workers, or were doing something else in Christian ministry. And it all started with a maid, an unknown young woman, who took little Tommy Bewes to hear Mr. Moody. She brought a young boy to the light and from that simple act the light has shown ever brighter throughout the whole world, wherever the descendants of Tommy Bewes have gone.

What If that young woman, that maidservant at the house, hadn't bothered? What if she had said, "I have only one evening off each week; I want to enjoy it by having fun with my friends"? Or, what if she believed that true change comes only by decisions made in Parliament? But she didn't. She was faithful. And she brought a young boy to the light. Look how that light has been shining ever since!

What Will God Say to Me?

What will God say to me if, before Him, I have to admit that I have covered the light? He sent his Son to be that light but I brought all my other views and opinions and politics and social concerns and piled them on top of the light. What will God say? And how will I answer?

I can argue, of course, that someone has to stand for morality in an immoral culture; someone has to point out how decadent we have become and how certain politicians are hurting the basic structure of what made our nation strong. But, I think, God might remind me that He knows all that. He is neither deaf nor blind

But neither is God deaf nor blind to our chasing after other lights of our own liking in the media or on the political grandstands. Did God call a William Wilberforce? He did, and used that faithful man to end a horror that was the human trafficking of slaves in England. But nowhere do we read that Wilberforce got personal delight, power surges of adrenalin or the pleasure of denouncing his opposition. He was humble, he was obedient, and he changed a nation.

Where are the humble ones, the obedient Christians, the people who are on their knees in the midst of the strident voices we hear declaring what they believe is politically or socially of God? When are Christians seeking the voice and leading of God?

Or are they only power-hungry brokers of a pseudo-Christianity that brings them much attention but covers over the light of Christ? What will they say to the Savior about what they have done in His name? How will they explain to Him that they have buried His redeeming message? They made a basket and under it they hid His light.

Time to Hold up the Light

Recently I read a story about something that happened at a youth camp. One evening, the kids were putting on a skit. A young girl came walking along pulling petals off a flower and reciting, "He loves me, He loves me not."

When she came to the last petal she exclaimed, "He loves me!"

A young man standing nearby asked, "Who loves you?"

She replied, "Jesus loves me."

He said, "Oh, I could have told you that."

To which she replied, "Then why didn't you?"

Let me ask, "When was the last time you spoke to a person about the Savior? When was the last time you tried? Why didn't you?"

On the one hand, when we take personal responsibility for lost souls as though it is all up to us, we deny the work of the Holy Spirit who seeks the lost and is the One who converts. We cannot do that work of God in and of ourselves. We trust God to do the work. If we think we are the soul winners all by ourselves, we could do more harm, pushing and driving people away from Christ.

But the opposite to that is to sit back, say it is all God's work and ignore the serious responsibilities that Jesus presented when He said, "Go into all the world..." (Mark 16:15). And "You are my witnesses" (Acts 1:8).

I don't think any of us wants to stand by while we see people going into a Christless eternity. We know the work is of God, but we also know that we work too, as God has instructed us to do. It may be something very simple but long lasting.

Think about someone you helped to hear the Gospel message. Maybe you have not seen that person in years. But perhaps God has been doing a work in that person's life and his descendants after him. N. T. Wright, Bishop of Durham and a New Testament scholar, says something about this. He wrote about the stone carver who may be asked to carve one stone while never knowing how it will be used in the building of a great cathedral.

And that may be what God is asking us to do when we bring the light of Christ to this person or to that one. We may not know where that shining will lead because we may not know all that the Holy Spirit is doing in that person's life.

As we go to people who are lost, we take a gift with us. It is the gift of life through Jesus. We are told in Scripture that a person can't come to the light unless the Father draws him (see John 6:44). So we pray that the Father will draw to Himself the people whom we know and see each day where we live and work. When we carry the light, we may not even have to talk about it. In the darkness, the light doesn't have to explain itself; it is seen because it shines.

It is said that years ago, when Charles Finney, an attorney who was also an evangelist, was witnessing to a man, the man's wife, hearing about it, said to her husband, "Why didn't you tell him to mind his own business." Her husband replied, "Had you been there you would have thought that it was his business."

It is our business too. We love God and we care about people too much not to make it our business to present the Good News of the Savior. The friends, the neighbors whom God has put in our way, are our responsibility.

God leads us; we don't have to fret about it being all our work. We don't have to feel driven. But we do have to realize that what we do with the light is important to God.

Jesus said that the fields are white unto harvest (see John 4:35). We have only one life to live and therefore we may have only one chance to reach the people whom God has brought to us. The harvest is all around us.

As we come alongside people and listen to them, we discover that they don't relate to our perfect lives; they relate to our real lives in which God has taken control. They see how a follower of Jesus lives. They can tell the difference. It's the light that they are seeing. That light always belongs on a lampstand; it doesn't belong under our clutter.

A Different Day for the Educated

There was a time when educated people knew the Bible because the Bible was part of their schooling. The uneducated may not have known Scripture; the well-educated did. For example, in one of his writings Mark Twain (Samuel Clemens) wrote, "His logic was like the peace of God." An educated person would have understood that comment immediately because he would have known the Scriptures. Today, very few would understand what Twain was saying.

The peace of God is "beyond human understanding." Twain didn't have to say it; people knew it. Today it would have to be explained that the man's logic was like the peace of God because the peace of God is beyond understanding—so was the man's logic. We are no longer able to write or say what Mark Twain wrote and said because we are not a biblically-educated people anymore.

Oh, we think we are educated. Gen X people and Millennials will boast that they have more information available to them then their grandparents ever had. They are right. But they may not have the ability to think through the meaning of what they have available to them as their grandparents could. Factoids aren't facts; one-liners don't contribute to depth of thought, and the continuous interruption caused by social media does not allow the mind to be reflective and pull information together to make sense of it.

As an editor and a teacher of writing, I have had to help writers create the simple article and even the simple sentence. With the constant motion of people's brains they have become less able to read or write a complete thought-containing sentence or to read or write an article that has more content to it and is more logical than their daily tweets or blogs.

Politicians and the media know that. Simple one-liners get the attention of voters. The explanation of policy and what that policy means do not. Television news producers know this as well. Warm fuzzy news features connect if they are brief; factual news stories are not so much appropriated. So instead of news we get entertainment in the name of news. But that's just the way it is because that's all so many people in our culture can handle. It is a new day, a different day even for the educated. They just don't know what is critical to eternal life. They don't even have a shallow grasp of it. We are the ones to show them what the message of Jesus means and do it in a way that every person can understand.

Knowing How People Learn

We who have Good News to communicate have to know how people learn. We have to understand what they can understand. If we are older Christians who are linear in our thinking, we have to move over to segmented thinking. A long sentence or complicated statement might not be followed or understood in our sound-bite and Twitter age. We don't dumb down the Gospel; we just break it into smaller pieces that our hearer can understand and grasp. It can be done if we are intentional about it. But if instead of learning how that other person understands we only want our hearer to come over to our style of learning, communication will probably never take place. And, for many Christians, communication with unbelievers isn't taking place.

I've watched an evangelist who takes his music and message around the world—the same music and the same message no matter where he goes. His thinking is that the human need is the same and the Holy Spirit is the same. So, he assumes, if his package connects with people in Andalusia, Alabama, it will connect equally as well in Ankara, Turkey. He doesn't understand that changing the presentation is not the same as changing the message. He isn't compromising anything by first learning about others before he proclaims his message. Sadly, there are many believers who act like that evangelist.

We are missionaries in our own land. Some of the best communicators of the Gospel are Christians who come to the U. S. from other countries. They have no preconceived notions about how to communicate. They have to learn the culture, the vocabulary and the learning style of Americans. That's what we would do too if we went to another culture.

That missionary's desire to understand how another person learns will serve us all. Assuming that another person will somehow automatically understand our own way of thinking is no different than a missionary who wants to import his communication package from his own culture and expect it to resonate elsewhere. It won't.

Am I listening? Am I hearing? Especially, can I hear and respond to the man or woman who lives in the secular world and is governed by a secular mind?

My wife, Andrea, had an aunt whom we would visit when she was in her late 90s. She couldn't hear well and couldn't see well. Over the years, Andrea had often spoken to her about the Savior until one day Aunt Connie said angrily, "Don't talk to me about religion." So we tried to respect her wishes.

But one day Andrea was somewhere else and Aunt Connie and I were alone together. That was a good opportunity to talk about her and the Savior. She had so little to go on that it was hard. She was a new-age person before it was popular. How could I communicate about the light and show her Jesus in a way that she could understand when she had no spiritual understanding to build on?

When I told Andrea about that visit, we found a large white card. On it, in big letters, we printed out John 3:16 and put her aunt's name in it and took it to her. It read, "For God so loved Connie, that He gave his one and only Son, that if Connie will believe in Him, she shall not perish but have eternal life." Aunt Connie traced the words with her finger, reading slowly and then said, "This has my name in it." That gave us another opportunity to tell her why her name was there.

In subsequent visits we saw that the card was propped up near her bed, placed where she could see it. Did she come to saving faith? Did she put her trust in the Savior? We don't know. We were never able to get a definitive reply. We could only show her the way.

We are to learn how the other person learns, hear what keeps that person from the Savior if we can, and show the light of the redeeming Christ. For a 97-year-old woman, we tried to find a way; for each person whom we meet we find different ways. But what comes first is showing the light—and doing all that we can to never cover it up.

There come those moments, when we engage others with the truth of God, that we will quickly see how our truth can be misinterpreted and its meaning changed. Truth is truth, but not everyone sees it as we do. We have to expect that.

chapter 9

All Truth Is God's Truth—but We May Be Missing It

I hear it all the time: "You have your truth; I have my truth." That's the teaching of our culture. "Your truth or my truth—both are equal. Don't try to ram your truth down my throat." And the culture has been getting away with that false notion because Christians have let them do it. We have let people believe that all truth is man's truth even the truth we declare comes from God. We have claimed our biblical truth with the emphasis on "our." And to the secular mind, "our" truth is of no greater value than "their" truth.

It seems that many who are believers in Jesus as the way, the truth and the life have bought into the secular view of your "truth, my truth." They have made biblical teaching "my truth" when, in fact, it is God's truth to be accepted or rejected but it isn't mine by my own making. I don't have "my individual truth" especially if it is truth given by God. When I let the secular person think that he has his truth and I have mine, I allow him to believe that even what I tell him is God-given truth is only something that I have come to and determined on my own.

But it doesn't end there. In a group discussion about an article in Atlantic Monthly (August 14, 2013), the group I was in landed on the words of the author, Mark Bowden. He was talking about the use of drones, but it was his conclusion that drew affirmations from the group. Bowden wrote, "Abiding carefully by the law—man's law, not God's—making judgments carefully, making them transparent and subject to review, is the only way to invest them with moral authority." So, came the conclusion, there is no moral authority except man's law; certainly not God's. But then, interestingly, the same members in that group also agreed that "Morality differs with each individual."

So I have my truth and you have yours; I have my morality and you have yours. Each of us has our own. What we need, we are told, is man's moral authority, not God's. And no one in the group that day seemed to consider the contradiction in what they were saying to each other. How can we have "man's moral authority" if each of us has our own individual moral authority? It seemed that all that mattered to the group affirming this was the individualism and the opposition to any moral authority that comes from God.

Jesus said, "Then you will know the truth, and the truth will set you free" But there is an "if" before those words: "If you hold to my teachings" (John 8:31–32). That's the part that is usually not quoted. When I surrender to the Savior, I respond to His truth. I am a follower of His truth, not my own. The apostle John put it this way, "I have no greater joy than to hear that my children are walking in the truth" (3 John 4). Truth, then, is not simply information. Truth is a Person. Christian followers of truth walk with that Person, who is Christ. Certainly our truth is not of our own making. But even some Christians think so because they have made it so. For some Christians, even biblical truth becomes personal; it is mine to accept, reject or change.

A Biblical Problem

When I'm editing a manuscript for an author and come to Scripture that the author is using, I find that I can run into difficulties. If he gives the version used and I check that version, I often find that some of the quote is accurate, some parts include other versions and some parts are the author's own words inserted into the biblical text. He doesn't quote God's truth; he quotes his own version of what he wants God's truth to be.

Where did we get the idea that we can violate Scripture to make it say what we want it to say and yet quote it as the authoritative word of God? Is there a belief among Christians that my word is just as inspired as God's word? Am I so unwilling to follow or teach what the Bible says that I will intentionally bend it to suit myself? If so, I prove to the secular "my truth, your truth" person that I am not willing to follow what God says but have to add or subtract from it, making it my truth, not God's. Why am I upset with someone who doesn't believe the Bible is the Word of God, who says he has his own truth, when I, who say I believe that the Bible is the Word of God, want to change it to make it express my own version of truth?

And if the secular person should look up what I am quoting from the Bible and find that I have not told the truth about God's word but have made it into my own word instead, why should he believe anything else that I say about God? He can quickly see that what I tell him isn't God's Word of Truth; it is only my version of truth.

Those who play fast and loose with Scripture not only make it obvious that they have no intention of obeying what God says, twisting what Scripture says to suit themselves, but that other people shouldn't believe them when they state, "The Bible teaches…" The Christian has just proven the secular person correct—you have your truth and I have mine.

If a Christian can't follow what God teaches, he has no right to assume that others who don't follow what God says are somehow more pagan. When the Bible states that, "All Scripture is

God-breathed and is useful for teaching, rebuking, correcting and training in righteousness..." (2 Tim. 3:16), it doesn't mean that we correct the Bible; it means that the Bible corrects us. We have no license to violate the Scriptures and then declare that our truth comes from God. Obviously, to any who listen to us, it doesn't.

Those Delicate Secularists

But if Christians will twist God's truth to suit themselves, secular people are not as open or as faithful to truth as they say they are. One evening we were watching the movie *Soul Surfer* and noticed something. There was a disclaimer given about the views of the people in the film. Those views were Christian views. My wife said, "We have to protect the delicate secular mind." She was right. Christians are not considered when a film contains content offensive to believers. The response is, "You don't have to watch." But a disclaimer is needed to protect the delicate secularist who can't handle the challenge of views other than his own—especially if they are Christian views. The secular person who thinks he is accepting of truth can be just as selective and self-protecting as anyone else about what truth he will listen to or be open to believe.

I love to interact with the secular person. Most are honest about their views, and the ones who are truly liberal are open to balanced and genuine persons of faith. The Gospel is new to many; it isn't that they have heard it before and rejected it. They haven't heard it. It isn't the truly liberal person who is difficult to talk to; it is the narrow-minded person who thinks he is liberal but won't listen to any view other than his own. He thinks he is broadminded; he isn't broadminded at all.

Yet too many Christians either criticize the secular person for his unbelief or fade away in fear of confrontation. We don't need to fear, and we fail the One who sent us into the world if all we do is attack or run away. Jesus may have been harsh toward religious people—we see that clearly enough in John 8—but Jesus was tender and kind to those who just didn't know the truth but were willing to engage with Him to learn that truth, whether it was the Samaritan woman at the well or the tax collector named Zaccheus.

When dealing with the secular mind, we need to take our instructions and our example from Jesus. I have found that having a genuine interest in the views of the other person goes a long way toward opening a presentation to the message of the Savior. Warmth attracts; cold causes pain. When I approach a person with warmth, I don't have to harshly tear off his protective coverings. Like a man standing in the warm sun, he will soon remove his coat of resistance on his own.

If a person has truth on his side, it can be acknowledged because ultimately all truth is God's truth. Where I see truth, I agree with it. That makes it much easier to engage a person when I encounter falsehood, at least the kind of falsehood that is neither true on a general level nor true biblically. Here, in the homosexuality debate, is an example of your truth, my truth and the problem of not hearing one another.

The Homosexual Example

When the Supreme Court made its decision about homosexual marriage, it was arguing over equal rights under the law. It was a legal issue. The secular person supports that. When Christians argue about homosexual marriage it is seen as a biblical issue. We know what Scripture says. So, when speaking to the secular person about homosexual marriage, we are talking past each other. Neither understands where the other is coming from. Also, because the secular person has a personal view of morality and the Christian has a biblical view of morality, the secular person assumes that we have chosen our biblical view just as he has chosen his secular view. He has no concept of the redeemed person following God's word. We can't expect that he should understand. So we need to listen to him and begin where he is and let his own arguments convince him when they fall apart. And, often, they will fall apart.

In the United States, where homosexuality has become a major political and social issue, I have no problem agreeing with the truth that the homosexual is a fellow human being who is worthy of every legal right of citizenship that belongs to every other citizen. And when the Supreme Court handled the issue, I had no difficulty in seeing that their approach was strictly legal, based on equal rights for all citizens. But I do have a different view than most of the culture on the practice of homosexuality. I have to yield to what God teaches in Scripture.

Sex was God's idea. He created man and woman to enjoy sex as He planned it. And through sex, we propagate the family. I can also state that I believe God put fences around sexual purity for our own sakes. I can point to biblical admonitions that believers try to follow. I can point to views of Christian marriage as they differ from views about secular marriage. I can advocate that homosexual men and women need the Savior as much as heterosexual men and women do.

I can be opposed to homosexual sex but also teach that sexual sin by heterosexuals is not to be practiced either. Neither homosexuals nor many heterosexuals are practicing what God planned. Two heterosexuals becoming just mating partners isn't the same as enjoying the sexuality of one to whom we are committed before God, one whom we love and who, by God's selection, complements us physically and emotionally. Two men can't do that. Neither can two women. But neither can a man and a woman who only know sex as the culture has degraded it to be. Take God out of the equation and we have nothing much different than what happens in a barnyard.

I hear Christians bemoaning the homosexual agenda, the militancy of those who don't simply want to practice their homosexuality but demand that Christians approve it. Vocal, strident homosexuals want us to deny the clear teachings of Scripture. They want tolerance, acceptance and approval of what is not tolerated, accepted or approved in God's Word. Homosexual militancy grows as the Supreme Court, looking at homosexuality from the legal side, sees the need for equality under the law. Christians, looking at homosexuality from the biblical side, still see that there is a conflict with the clear teachings of Scripture.

We as Christians seem to want homosexuals to behave the way we want them to behave. But how can those whose minds have not been transformed by Christ act like those who are people of the transformed mind? How can those without the Gospel truth act as those who do have that truth? We live in a fallen, broken world. We can't be critical of broken people acting like broken people. They have nothing else. As one seminary professor told a gay, lesbian and transgender audience, "You aren't gay; you are miserable. And I'm not straight. I am twisted by sin. Both of us need the Savior to make us whole people."

But Christians too often become angry and hateful toward those who are angry and hateful toward them. We behave as though we should act as militantly as they do, not as people who understand that God knows our fallen world much better than we do. God has put us in this fallen world to be salt and light.

One day I was reading a paper put out by homosexuals for homosexuals. I don't recall how I happened to see it, but it was very revealing. In it the writer was stating that homosexuals blame their overuse of alcohol, drugs and their high percentage of suicide on the pain caused by those "homophobes" who hate them. Then the writer went on to say that if the society ever accepts homosexuality and no longer pays attention to it or calls it an aberration, practicing homosexuals are going to have to face their own demons without the easy excuse that what they feel brings them so much pain is caused by someone else. The writer said that homosexuals were going to have to be honest and admit that they are their own enemies, something they haven't had to do because of the ease of blaming others for their pain.

One man, one woman, is the cry of the Christians. But those who disagree with us point to the failure of so many one-man, one-woman marriages. Film stars jump in and out of marriages five and six times. Radio commentator Rush Limbaugh, whom Christians seem to enjoy quoting as someone whose ideas they approve, has had four wives. Rupert Murdoch's third divorce was from a woman 39 years his junior, and he picked up immediately with a young massage therapist. Around us we see people treating marriage as little more than a brief honeymoon and then it is over. We see multiple marriages without any thought of what marriage means and even multiple adulterous liaisons within marriage. And if the divorce rates are dropping in our country, it is only because fewer are marrying in the first place. People are just living together.

Living together is becoming the new norm; never mind what the results of that practice turn out to be in the inner being of each person. Is that what is meant by one man, one woman—any number will do so long as it is one marriage or one cohabitating couple at a time? As long as we go along with "my truth, your truth" we will have little to say to the culture about the pain so many feel that is caused by their twisted homosexuality or their twisted heterosexuality. The more we personally engage in biblical Christianity, the more the blessing of God will be seen as truth. It will be a contrast to the culture around us that cannot be denied.

So, society wonders, if multiple heterosexual marriages are not what God calls for but people engage in them all the time anyway, what is wrong with homosexual marriages even though that too is not what God calls for? Add to that all of the legal ramifications of marriage, the rights that married couples have under the law, and why the courts had to support equal rights for every citizen, and we have the mix that we face today. For Christians, are multiple heterosexual relationships somehow more "correct"? Are they better than homosexual relationships because at least with the heterosexuals, they are "one man, one woman" at any one time?

My Unaccepted Point of View

My own view isn't subscribed to by homosexuals. But neither has it been picked up by heterosexuals. To me, Christian marriage is one Christian man and one Christian woman united before God. Anything else can be called a union or marriage or another name, but it isn't Christian marriage. Christians practice Christian marriage even though the culture, whether it is heterosexual or homosexual, does not.

I'm convinced that we ought to have the legal side of marriage and the biblical aspect of marriage kept separate. Let all persons, no matter who they are, marry in a civil, legal proceeding in the offices of a magistrate. Then the playing field is legally level for all. The legal rights of a partner benefit all couples.

Then, let those who want to be married in the sight of God arrange a Christian marriage ceremony where the couple can gather with family and friends in the church, exchange their vows before God and man and make their pledges to each other and to God. Only those who are serious about obeying God in marriage will do it. But then clergy can say to all who ask, "We perform Christian marriage between two committed believers—man and woman." If someone wants anything else, he can have it anyway in the civil part that takes place in a secular setting.

In Christian marriage, there is offered solid counseling explaining what marriage is in the sight of God. There we learn that there are three in a Christian marriage: the man, the woman and God. It is a triangle. As the man moves closer to God at the top of the triangle, and as the woman moves closer to God at the top of the triangle, they draw closer to each other at the same time. Without that, two people might come together on the base plane but God is not a part of what they do, no matter what they call it.

Then we are no longer demanding that the culture change its ways to make us comfortable when the secular culture can't do it. Only the redeemed can behave as the redeemed; only light can act like light. Darkness can behave only like darkness. We are wrong to expect anything else. We are wrong to insist that the culture try to practice what only those who have new life in Christ are able to practice.

The culture may disagree with my views, but only a few persons with closed minds will argue that I am therefore homophobic. I can work with the homosexual, eat with the homosexual, join in sports with the homosexual and be neighbors with the homosexual. But that does not mean that I will engage in sex with a homosexual nor encourage him to do so in my attempts to not be seen as less than accepting of his views. But I won't accept or engage in extra-marital heterosexual relationships either. I have a Christian marriage. Before God, I am committed only to the one whom God gave me and who I married in the presence of God. The richness of that love relationship is something that the secular culture, homosexual or heterosexual, has no understanding of. It is a gift from God.

In a culture that speaks of being accepting of all beliefs, the secular person who can't handle my Christian convictions may not see that he is hypocritical, but he is. He can't say that all truth is equal if he rejects my Christian truth. Just knowing that helps me to engage in discussions with him being fully aware that given enough time he will reveal to himself his own hypocrisy regarding what is truth. I won't have to do it.

Science: Discoveries of Truth That Is Already There

Whether it is the discoveries of an Albert Einstein and his famous formula or a Frances Collins and the human genome project, science lauds itself for its discoveries, and properly so. It takes diligence to pursue those discoveries. But we make a mistake if we think that the discovery of something that is there is the same as putting it there. When spacecraft explore the outer regions of our solar system, and even break out into another system, they are sending back information about what is there. When someone finds a new world in the micro-universe of the human body, he is discovering what is there to be found. He didn't put it there.

God is truth. He is all truth. When a scientist discovers something new in the macrocosm or the microcosm, he didn't create it and place it there. When he comes up with a "truth," what he has discovered is God's truth. I have listened to lectures by scientists who are opening new and wonderful worlds of discovery. They practically twist into pretzel shapes in order to somehow talk about the marvel of what God has done without referring to God. I feel sorry for them. Their lives would be so much easier if they could just bring themselves to explain the unexplainable with God as the giver of the truth they have just discovered. Instead, trying to find alternative words to use, they skirt along the edge of God and end up with a universe in which they explain, "It just happened."

If the discoverer of scientific truth has trouble acknowledging that he can discover only what is already there to be discovered and that God put it there, it would be hoped that if he turned to a Christian believer for an understanding of God and His truth he would get an honest answer. Too often what he gets from us is a dishonest answer. We exchange what God says is His truth for what we say is our truth and then the other person can once again assume that he is correct—that indeed we each do have our own truth and one person's truth is as good as another's.

Battles over Speculation

One day at a conference I was walking quickly to a class where I was to teach when a small group sitting together in a corner waved me over. They said they had been discussing evolution and asked me, "Do you think we are descended from apes?" I replied, "No, I think we are descended from the geranium," and hurried on to the class I was teaching.

I wonder what that group thought. I hear the scientific evidence that points to all the similarities between humans and apes; there is plenty to look at, including DNA and its RNA (Ribonucleic acid) copies. But then we can find some similarities with geraniums too. The searching continues.

In a simple explanation, William Harris writing in *Are Humans Really Descended from Apes?* answers the question, "If apes 'turned into' humans then apes should no longer exist." Harris says, "...the bottom-line rebuttal is simple—humans didn't descend from apes. That's not to say humans and apes aren't related, but the relationship can't be traced backward along a direct line of descent, one form morphing into another."

Today's scientists look more at change than evolution. Charles Darwin wrote of *The Evolution of the Species,* but that's not really what Darwin was working with. He was working with changing species, which is different than evolution of species. There are divergences, cross or interbreeding with some species going off from one another. It is much more complicated than Darwin would have guessed.

If we look at apes and man and geraniums, we are going to find, to one degree or another, similar compositions of the elements of the earth. I enjoy repeating the old joke about a scientist discussing creation with God. The scientist says, "You made man from the dust of the ground. Big deal, I can do that."

God replies "Go ahead."

The scientist reaches down to grab a handful of dirt when God says, "Wait a minute; make your own dirt."

We need to listen carefully to others. Then the person who wants to argue from "science" will see that often his science isn't real science anyway. Today's discoveries may build on or change yesterday's discoveries. I remember reading about a man visiting an Islamic Madrasa, where religion is taught. The teacher was asked if he taught any science. "Yes," the teacher replied. "We have a science book here on the shelf." The visitor examined the book. It was published in 1932.

We can't argue that the Bible is intended to be a scientific book. It isn't. It is a book about man and God. That doesn't change no matter what new scientific findings are made tomorrow. We know that God created all things. How He did it is beyond us; we can discover only bits and pieces. We make a mistake if we think one piece of information is the whole explanation of creation and we make a mistake if we try to make the Bible into a book that can totally explain to us the workings of the God who is other.

Evangelicals tend to get into fringe battles over speculation. We get pushed into a corner on some scientific issue such as evolution and don't recognize that God is always God no matter what is discovered. The world tells us that evangelicals are being shaken in their faith. We learn that half of young evangelicals lose their faith by the time they turn 18 years old and start college, especially if they attend a secular university. I don't know what degree of faith those teens once had but I can tell people that I had the opposite experience. I turned from unbelief to faith in Christ while a student at a secular university.

Creationism as a Truth in Public Schools

Religion is based on man's attempts to reach up to God. Christianity is based on God's act of reaching down to man. We see it in Philippians chapter two that describes the self-emptying of God. Anything else that becomes a religion accepted by faith is an "ism." These come and go over time. As one person explained, "Sooner or later every 'ism' becomes a 'wasim.'"

On one occasion I was listening to a man who was expressing his views that the Bible's teaching about creation should not be taught in public schools. He referred to it in a derogatory way as "creationism." In one sense I agree with him because I don't want a teacher who doesn't believe the Bible teaching the Bible. I'd rather have no Bible teaching in school than a perverted teaching of the Bible. But his point was that there is the biblical view of creation and there is science. I showed him that what we really have is creationism and scientism. Both are religious views taken by faith.

To the person who tells me that it is wrong to teach biblical creation in public school, I tell him I agree. I don't want the Bible taught in public school and I don't want the Koran taught in public school. But neither do I want the religion of scientism taught in public school. Honest scientists will say, "We don't know for certain but our theories give us a basis for exploring and making various discoveries." But many older scientists, especially retired ones who haven't kept up with what has been happening in the world of science over the past 10 or 12 years, tend to take by faith what is theory. They make theory into fact and denounce any other view that doesn't agree with their faith position. Theory is theory. If we make a fact out of it, we are creating a faith position. That's not science; that's scientism, which is a religion accepted by faith. So there is faith-based religion and there is faith-based science. Those who lay claim to science and insist that they don't live by faith deceive themselves. It is not a matter of faith and non-faith. It is really a matter of faith in who or what.

Where we run into problems is when the science-faith people and the creation-faith people will not look at the other person's position. When that happens, it is the Christian who often loses because he has the most invested in his faith. Seeing that, the secularist holds onto his science-religious faith because he sees Christians holding onto their religious views without evidential facts to back up either position. It's a stalemate. I can't prove the existence of God; I can only show the works of God in the world. The secular person can't prove much of his science faith either— certainly the parts that can't be replicated—only the results he sees from it. The honest person accepts what is proven and true and admits that what is not yet proven as true has to be taken on faith.

We misunderstand faith and we misunderstand science and we argue with each other about what most people in the rest of the world—whether believers in faith-based scientism or faith-based creationism—aren't arguing very much about at all. Something that is bigger than our faith-science arguments is taking place in the world. God is breaking out of our small boxes of faith-versus-science positions that seem so important to us, especially if we refuse to look beyond our own narrow world view.

The universe, whether macro or micro, is much more complex than we once thought, and we are in awe at how everything works together. The most recent discoveries have exploded misconceptions that were held as absolute truth by scientists as recently as five years ago. Most people who make science their religion do so not because they know so much but because they haven't kept up with what is being discovered and, in truth, do not know much at all. I take delight in the title that the November 2, 2013, issue of *The Economist* gave to recent studies of dark matter and dark energy. The title read, "Absence of evidence, or evidence of absence?"

It Isn't about Winning Arguments

Engaging with another person in a discussion about God's truth isn't about winning an argument. There is no winning to be had. It is about letting that person speak of his truth openly to me. He will, in time, see where his "truth" falls apart, not because I am a clever person with my arguments but because God's truth is what it is and we are made to be in need of that truth. My chief responsibility is to be faithful to that truth of God as revealed in Scripture and is available to others as well.

Our problems with the secular mind will come not because a person is thoroughly liberal. A true liberal is a person who is open. The problem is that so many who consider themselves liberal are not liberal at all but are extremely closed-minded. Arguing with a person will never bring him to see his lack of liberal thinking; openly drawing him out will more likely reveal to him his lack of liberal thinking. A true liberal, a truly open-minded person, may not be far from the kingdom.

Unfortunately, I have found that the opposite is not usually as true. A true conservative is secure in his beliefs and isn't threatened by those who argue against them. A false conservative is not. There are many conservatives who cannot be exposed to any ideas other than their own. They will reinforce their ideas by talking only to others of like mind and reading or listening only to reporters who give them information that they want, even sometimes false information that reinforces their conservative beliefs. They are closed to even thinking about anything else.

Listening To a Self-described Liberal

I appreciate a psychology professor like Jonathan Haidt whom I would consider to be a true and honest liberal. For 16 years he was professor of psychology at the University of Virginia and is now the Thomas Cooley Professor of Ethical Leadership at New York University's Stern School of Business. He points out the lack of fairness and balance in many academic liberals. He takes the example of a college campus ministry, such as InterVarsity Christian Fellowship, that will place only believers in positions of leadership even though they are open as a group to any person who wants to attend their meetings. Haidt points out that those academicians who condemn such practices by the Christians on campus are doing the same thing themselves. Even though the university may be open to all students, the university is not open about who can serve on the faculty or in the administration. What they condemn in the campus Christian groups is what they practice themselves among the administration and faculty. They require strict credentials for their leadership. Haidt is a liberal who sees the hypocrisy among other liberals who can search only for the speck in another person's eye.

If I can enter into discussions with those who are secular but are seeking after truth, I may still have problems with the picture that has been given to them by other Christians who are not open to discussions but who want only to lash out in anger at what they see as a secular attack on their faith. So I often ride two horses. I talk with the secular people about those who are people of faith and I talk with people of faith about secular people. Too often, neither understands the other and, too often, they don't want to. I need to be bilingual if I want to have an effective witness to both believers and unbelievers.

Abortion, Death Panels, Guns and God

The secular person may tell us that he approves of abortion and selected death for the elderly. The Christian is opposed to both because he believes in the sanctity of life. But the truth is that in many cases neither believes in the sanctity of life. The Christians, who too often have pro-gun people in their ranks, are pro killing whether they want to admit to it or not. The evidence about guns and death is in nearly every nightly news report. In Britain, where guns are not allowed, people don't have guns, and killings drop every year—and they were not very high to begin with. In the U.S., gun-related deaths seem to increase and multiple shootings are growing. The argument that when good people don't have guns only criminals will have guns doesn't hold up in places like the United Kingdom.

In the U. S., the Christians want the secular person to respect life; the secular person wants the Christian to respect life. The Christian is labeled as wanting guns without control. It doesn't matter that babies are gunshot in the womb and elderly people are gunshot while innocently sitting on their porches. That seems to be all right with many vocal Christians as long as abortive drugs or medical instruments don't kill those babies and end-of-life measures are protected from what are referred to as "death panels." At Liberty University in Lynchburg, Virginia, a male student was permitted to carry a concealed weapon to class. But he couldn't step into the lobby of a woman's dorm. One young man did, and he was shot and killed, according to a November 21, 2013, Faith Report on Christian radio.

"You don't care about life," says the Christian. "Neither do you," says the secular person. But the secular person isn't concerned about obeying Jesus. The Christian is. And as long as the secular person sees the Christian's inconsistency with his selective pro-life stand, the Christian has no message about being pro-life and having the mind of Christ.

We want the liberal-minded person to be fair, but we don't always act fairly with him. Who is the one who is vocally pro-life yet proves that he doesn't believe in the sanctity of life at all by preferring guns over life? We who call ourselves conservatives will say one thing about the sanctity of life and then deny that we truly are pro-life by our actions. Abortion is wrong, assisted suicide of the terminally ill is wrong, but carrying a gun in order to shoot someone who doesn't look right to us is acceptable. The secular person sees us quite accurately.

We will even slice and dice the Constitution to cut out the words in it about a well-regulated militia in order to promote our gun ownership. Is every owner of an AK 47 or a Glock handgun a member of a well-regulated militia? We will twist the Second Amendment rather than fairly read it for what it says and realize the context in which it was written at the founding of our country. Those who want guns are not interested in what the Founding Fathers intended. They want their own interpretation of this amendment so they can have their weapons but not be subject to the discipline of a "well-regulated militia." When someone tells me he is pro-Second Amendment, I ask him to quote it to me. He usually can't. He hasn't read what it says.

Is the 14th Amendment Also to Be Upheld?

Both the "your truth" and the "my truth" people stumble over the 14th Amendment. When the Roe v. Wade decision came down from the Supreme Court in 1973, Christians roared against abortion. They argued about it. Except that from the court's perspective it was more about a woman's right to privacy under the due process clause of the 14th Amendment than it was an approval of killing babies. In fact, there was a concern about limiting abortions that also required a balance with the woman's right to health care. The ruling also stepped into the ongoing debate between federal law and states' rights.

But some of us are so busy arguing the abortion side that we forget what the broader ruling was about in the first place. So supporters of Roe v. Wade are thinking about privacy and a woman's right to proper health care; the Christian conservatives are thinking about killing babies. The two sides are rarely communicating. Too often we prefer to argue with anger rather than come to a friend or neighbor with our understanding of both sides, see where we may be on the same page, and then bring in our Christian position at that point rather than screaming from one side of the street and pushing everyone who disagrees with us over to the other side of the street. Rather than look for truth, we seem to have a need to put people into boxes and then hate them for being in the boxes where we put them.

Truth and the Sanctity of Life

Does pro-life apply everywhere or it is just for Americans? Here is an example that I have hesitated to mention until now. For me it is a painful story. It is an example of my believing what another said was his truth only to discover later that it was not what I had assumed his truth to be.

I voted for George W. Bush for president. I am pro-life; I believe in the sanctity of life and, when I voted, I believed that George W. Bush believed in the sanctity of life too. But I found out that I was wrong, and when I learned about the abortions that happened during his presidency I became disturbed by the thought that I was responsible because of my vote for him. My wife had to remind me that I was not the only person who voted George W. Bush into office.

Why was I so troubled? In a news story published December 13, 2009, I saw that, "Under President George W. Bush, the United States withdrew from its decades-long role as a global leader in supporting family planning, driven by conservative ideology that favored abstinence and shied away from providing contraceptive devises in developing countries, even to married women."

The U.S. had been contributing to the United Nations Population Fund (UNFRA). But that was halted. In 2007, Ejike Oji, of Nigeria, testified before the U.S. Foreign Affairs Committee that this action contributed to unsafe abortions. Thousands of women were losing their lives.

One woman in Uganda has borne 13 children. She didn't want to have that many children but it was important to her husband to father a large family. She can't feed the children she has in the poverty-stricken country where they live. Did she want to bring yet another child into a family that can't feed the children they already have? So she sought for birth control that was once provided by America to help poor women prevent future pregnancies so that they could care for the children they already had, but under President Bush that contraception was no longer available.

What will a woman in that situation do? Will she go to a back-alley abortionist, risking her own life to do it? Surely cutting off contraceptive aid will contribute to abortions in larger numbers. Studies show that one in five pregnancies worldwide ends in abortion. President Bush could continue to declare that he was anti-abortion and pro-life in America and in doing so garner votes like mine. But we who voted for him learned too late that we were quite certainly contributing to increased abortions in the poverty-stricken areas of the world.

We have all seen the pictures of starving babies elsewhere in the world. A woman who is unable to feed her babies finds herself pregnant again because her husband rules over her and she no longer has any personal access to free birth control. What will she do? If we are appalled by back-alley abortions in our country where there is still medical help available if something should go wrong, what would a back-alley abortion be like for a Ugandan woman?

That once-free contraceptive help was no longer available. When President Bush cut the funding did he know that he would contribute to more abortions, not fewer? Did he write that off as unimportant so long as American babies weren't being aborted? Is contraception for American women who can afford it themselves and who can vote pro-life more important than contraception for African women who can't afford it and can't vote in our elections?

My reaction of being hurt by what was going on doesn't strike a similar chord with many of my fellow believers. They tend to take only the first part, the pro-life in America part, and choose to ignore the larger world. Is that what God would have us do? Are poor African women of less value than American women? Are babies born in other countries nonentities? Can we as believers take such divided stands and still hold our heads up about being pro-life?

Pro-life to me goes beyond abortion. To me being pro-life means a belief in the sanctity of life even when it comes to the execution of prisoners convicted of murder. We need to be very careful about those executions. There may be a need for the death penalty for murder, but sometimes we apply it unfairly and often in a surprisingly cavalier manner. In spite of so many examples that have been shown of the wrong prisoners being on death row for a crime committed by somebody else, George W. Bush, while governor of Texas, saw his state execute 152 prisoners, more than any other governor in modern history until surpassed by his successor, the pro-life advocate Rick Perry. When Perry ran for president, Texas had already racked up 234 executions. Is this a pro-life position that Christians can approve? How does the secular person think this through as he looks at those of us who declare ourselves to be Christians and pro-life?

Pro-life touches another area of life and death. Mercury, sulfur dioxide, nitrogen oxide and other pollutants coming from our factories contribute to the illness and death of many young children. Our infant mortality rate is higher than most other developed countries and even higher than some of the underdeveloped countries. But putting caps on factory chimneys, scrubbing out the pollutants before they enter the air we breathe, costs money. That money, if invested in clean factories, would mean less money in the pockets of the business owners and stockholders.

George H.W. Bush signed a new Clean Air Act in November 1990. His son, George W. Bush, initiated the Clear Skies Act of 2003 providing for what was called an "alternative regulatory classification." As explained by Wikipedia, the act was "...a market-based cap-and-trade approach which intends to legislate power plant emissions caps without specifying the specific method used to reach those caps. The Initiative would reduce the cost and complexity of complaints and the need for litigation."

What did this do for infant deaths? Read the statistics and where we continue to rank in the world when it comes to infant mortality. What did this do for the wallets of the CEOs and other executives of these plants since they could now decide for themselves, without strict regulation, how to interpret the law and what they would or would not do to clean up the pollutants from their factories?

Following my conscience, and believing in the sanctity of life, I voted for a president who I then found contributed to the destruction of life. I did not check out what his truth meant to him. It wasn't the biblical truth that I learned in Scripture about the value of life. Truth about the sanctity of life is not wobbly truth. It applies to all human life. I'm learning to check what I read and hear to see if the words written or spoken by someone mean what I think they mean.

Judged by a Different Standard

Our tendency toward Christian inconsistency has not been missed by the unbelievers around us. Because I am a follower of Jesus, because I say I am pro-life, it is assumed that I therefore am not really pro-life but only selectively believe in the sanctity of life. It is assumed that I am not an honest pro-life person but that I paste together my beliefs about what is pro-life and what is not. It is assumed that I put profit ahead of clean air and factory-operating costs ahead of the lives of infants. The moment I say that I am a follower of Jesus, I separate myself from those who are not, and I cannot be half in and half out with my pro-life beliefs. It is all for Jesus or not at all. That's the way secular people see it, and they are correct.

One writer noted the "Christian morals" when so many supported George W. Bush as the compassionate conservative who managed as governor to arrange tax cuts to the most affluent in Texas, at one point justifying money for oil and gas interests saying, "These are tough times for the oil and gas industry." Yet, in Texas, there seems to have been little money to subsidize health insurance for children from poor working families. At the turn of the 21st century, *The New York Times* reported, "Texas has had one of the nation's worst public health records for decades." Apparently oil and gas industrialists did very well. Those who received those benefits also added millions to the Bush election coffers.

Who Hurts Us Most?

How far will I go with being pro-life? Will I include the connection between war dead and war profits? When I voted for George W. Bush, the ballot included Dick Cheney for vice president. So he received my vote too. Later, as I followed his push to take the country toward war in Iraq and I saw how much personal profit Vice-President Cheney was making off that war, I turned into an even more depressed voter. It didn't help me when I read the comments of former Navy Secretary James Webb where he described the war in Iraq as "...the greatest strategic blunder in modern memory."

I was troubled too upon learning that one of the early acts of the Bush presidency was to take contracts from the realm of open bidding, that of awarding contracts to the lowest bidder as was done during the Clinton presidency, and giving those contracts to favorite corporations. Many went to Halliburton (KBR) where Dick Cheney had been CEO. The company continued to pay him an average of $150,000 per year while he was vice president. Was that legal? Was it a payoff for all the government contracts he was securing for Halliburton? The company claimed that the money was "deferred payments." With contracts in hand for many of the services in Iraq, including the rebuilding of infrastructure and the supply of gasoline, and even four million meals that were never served to the troops, Halliburton and its subsidiaries made 39.5 billion dollars during one decade of the Iraq war not only from the regular charges they made but the overcharges they collected that were sometimes so over-inflated that Congress had to look into them. So, even though his own holdings in Halliburton were in a blind trust and couldn't be manipulated by the vice president himself, the value of his holdings still went up 3,000 percent because of all the profit the company was making from the war.

I expected to hear my Christian friends complain about our vice president getting wealthy from a questionable war where so many people were dying. They didn't. Rather, the only negatives that I heard coming from Christians came when it was revealed that Cheney's daughter was a lesbian. For many Christians, being a lesbian was bad. Her father getting rich off a war where so many American soldiers died was not bad because, after all, he was a conservative and a Republican and therefore he belonged to the correct political party.

So the daughter, who is not responsible for anyone's death and who did not use high office to create a situation in Iraq where millions in personal profits could be made, is considered by many Christians to be less moral than her father. The secular world takes note. They see us for what we support and therefore want no part of us or the Savior we claim to follow. For many in the secular world who hear our words and see our actions, Christians are not a moral people. It is very difficult to approach the person who is watching us with the biblical message of redemption in Christ. Yet it is that message Jesus sent us into the world to proclaim. We have truth; we don't always demonstrate that truth. We are a people who need to return to God's truth both in what we believe and by how we live.

Selected Pieces of "My Truth"

Recently I was sent a copy of a newsletter containing a speech given at a Christian college forum. The speech was a cut-and-paste listing of all the evils caused by liberals and others branded as unbelievers in America. I read it eagerly, looking for something new, something that might prove that my concerns for the Christians who seem to buy into half-truths and outright lies would prove me wrong. But all the arguments presented were the same well-worn points put together like a patchwork quilt so that the whole was horrifying to consider.

On the one hand, Christians are viewed by secular liberals as troublesome, retrograde and reactionary. On the other hand, Christians insist that "liberals" are attacking religion. Are they? Or have we created our own case about that too? Notre Dame political science professor David Campbell speaks of a "grace gap in our country." Showing how far left people have gone, Campbell explained that among those who say grace daily (at meals), 40 percent identify as Democrats and 51 percent as Republicans. That was enough for him to prove that religious people who say grace at meals tend to the political right and are more likely to vote Republican.

According to this way of thinking, 51 percent of us say grace daily and therefore we belong to the religious right and are more likely to vote Republican. But 40 percent of us who say grace daily belong to the liberal left and therefore we are more likely to be Democrats.

That causes me to wonder; is a Democrat who prays before meals still politically left? Is a Republican who doesn't pray before meals still a right-wing voter? Is there no room for Democrats who pray and Republicans who don't pray to still work together as Americans? Or are we classified as fitting only into one camp or the other? Do those who teach these views enjoy being divisive?

We Do Not Select Our Own Truth

Christians are not the only ones who select their truth, be it about abortion, homosexuality or corporate profits built on the lives of hurting families. The secular person is just as guilty of manipulating his truth.

It is interesting to me that many who speak against belief in God and about the dangers of "religion" do not give credit to God for the mind that they use to defame His Name. There is a common grace that comes from God. The earth provides the sustenance that people need regardless of how they feel about God. The sun shines on the just and the unjust. According to the psalmist, "The heavens declare the glory of God" whether or not we want to admit it. Some do not. "For since the creation of the world God's invisible qualities—his eternal power and divine nature— have been clearly seen" (Rom. 1:20). But what have they done with what God has revealed to them? "...they neither glorified him as God nor gave thanks to him but their thinking became futile and their foolish hearts were darkened" (v. 21).

So the mind, a gift from God, is directed against the message of the saving grace of God who would have all persons come to faith in Christ. The love that draws but is slapped away comes from the Source of the brainpower that is used to deny God. The gift of common grace is used to reject the gift of saving grace. And those who do the rejecting do not even realize how they have been given their ability to reject the One who gave them that ability.

Truth calls for a different way to behave. I cannot select my truth, as many secular people tend to do. But neither can I as a Christian be two people, gorging on good Bible teaching, praising God, fellowshipping with believers, while at the same time berating "those pagans" who have their own version of truth because they have never met the God of all truth.

Truth for the Wise

In James 3, I read about wisdom and where it comes from. I learn how truth behaves and how it doesn't behave. There is a preface to the teaching that begins with a question: "Who is wise and understanding among you?" Presumably, there are those who are not wise and do not understand. But for those who do, James continues, "...the wisdom that comes from heaven is first of all pure; then peace-loving, considerate, submissive, full of mercy and good fruit, impartial and sincere" (v. 17).

In his book *Can Man Live without God?* Ravi Zacharias makes a clear and decisive statement: "...truth, by definition, will always be exclusive." Truth is truth. It stands. We may talk about "my own version of truth," but that personal view of truth doesn't change what is true. Too many in our culture are like children playing at the feet of their parents. No matter what imaginary worlds the children make up in their play, their parents remain in the real world. God remains in the real world no matter what games we children create in our fantasies.

Wisdom comes from knowing truth. I can't create my own truth. It comes from God. When wisdom that is built on God's truth rules, it isn't cluttered with all kinds of cultural or political content. It is pure. It doesn't call us to argumentative or disagreeable or nasty behavior; it is peace loving. When truth and its resulting wisdom is evident in a Christian's life, that person will never have to go around bragging that he has truth. It will be evident because God who is truth is living and acting in that person, producing the results that James describes. A life of truth is a life lived ready for God's new tomorrow.

chapter 10

Ready for Tomorrow

One day I was visiting with a man who said, "I'm not interested in Jesus as Savior. But He was a good teacher and I do follow His teachings." I asked him what that meant and he explained that he had spent 46 years as a church member and had a high view of the teachings of Jesus but not His divinity. Then, as though trying to show me just how much he believed Jesus, he said, "I believe all the teachings of Jesus."

"Oh, I replied." Then I took out my New Testament and read to him John 14:6 where Jesus said, "I am the way and the truth and the life. No one comes to the Father but through me." I asked, "Do you believe that?"

"No." he said.

So I simply pointed out to him that, "You believe all of the teachings of Jesus except the teachings of Jesus that you don't believe." He just shrugged. But it was a thought to leave with him until our next visit. He is a good example of the unexplored, the acceptance of a position that is not thought through. We, as believers, are to be a people who think through what we believe and help others to do the same. We who are in Christ have a message that others need to hear. We don't have to be afraid to do it. Whatever we have done in the past, even if we have hidden the light of Christ from the world, we can face a new tomorrow with a new confidence and make every day count for Christ.

Living in a Bigger World

When we as believers in Christ see what is happening in the larger world and move out from behind our American Christian trappings and our sometimes too-easily-accepted views that too often we refuse to examine, we see that there are new and refreshing winds blowing that promise a new tomorrow for the followers of Jesus. This new tomorrow isn't based on escape through the rapture, though we all look forward to that day. It is based on a higher trust in God who is above the minimalized world in which so many of us once tended to operate.

Alive and Well

I agree with Samuel Rodriquez, president of the National Hispanic Christian Leadership Conference. He wrote in an article that was printed in *alife,* June 1, 2013, "The obituary of American Christianity in the 21st Century already permeates both Church and society. Scholars and readers from within and outside the Church have concluded that Christianity in America will not survive the 21st Century in any viable or sustainable manner." Then he stated what I have also found to be true, "The Church of Jesus Christ is alive and well."

Could that be so, some ask. Do we, with Rev. Rodriquez, believe that "...the 21st century stands poised to experience the greatest transformative Christian movement in our history"? He continued, "This movement will affirm biblical orthodoxy, reform the culture, transform our political discourse, revolutionize the marketplace and usher in a New Awakening. I am convinced that the best is yet to come....What is the agenda for this new movement? It is not the agenda of the Democrat or the Republican, of the donkey or the elephant. This movement is driven by nothing other than the agenda of the Lamb."

Affirmation of Biblical Orthodoxy

One of the benefits of living in an openly secular culture—that was not as true when we were living in a nominally Christian culture—is that the difference between true and false, light and darkness, is far more obvious. People can tell the difference between the two. To bring society to that place where the difference is obvious requires that the church move out of its semi-Christian behavior, stop copying the culture in ideas, social behavior and even our media-influenced way of thinking and become what the church is—a New Covenant people. Look what happens when just one person wants to do things God's way.

Years ago, when I was serving as a pastor in a small community, there was another smaller church a few miles away that couldn't afford a pastor. I was asked to serve there every second Sunday afternoon. I was pleased to do it. There were about 35 people in that church, mostly from a few families.

But there was another man in that community who had not been part of the church because he wasn't a believer. That changed when he came to saving faith in Christ. He committed himself to the church and to the development of Christian maturity. He started seriously reading the Bible. One day, in an adult Sunday school class, he asked a question about tithing. It was a new concept to him and he wanted others in the church to help him understand how it was done.

This became an embarrassment to the people because most of them were not tithing nor were they interested in doing so. A few dollars in the offering plate per family seemed quite sufficient to them. But this man who asked about tithing was growing in the faith and, as we took hold of his question and explored tithing with the church members, we also talked about the value of systematic giving, having a budget and giving to missions.

That created a ruckus and 17 members left the church. We had only 35 to start. But it turned out to be a real revival. Those remaining members got serious about their faith. Then, others seeing the difference in them, wanted to know the Christ they obeyed. In the years to come that little church grew, built a new and larger building and gave systematically to missions. One man was used of God to turn a church around. One man introduced a new day.

That kind of "revival" may need to come to Christian churches today. People who have been on the edges of the faith will have to be all in or not in at all. It is time for believers to become a set-apart people, being what the apostle Peter meant when he said, "But you are a chosen people, a royal priesthood, a holy nation, God's special possession, that you may declare the praises of him who called you out of darkness into his wonderful light (1 Pet. 2:9). But first some changes have to come. It starts with being and living as orthodox as we claim to be.

Reform the Culture

How will our culture be reformed? How did that reform happen in the past? Look at the surrounding culture of the early church. Idol worship, sexual gods and goddesses worshiped in temples of debauchery, a heavy-handed foreign occupation force, slavery, extreme poverty alongside extreme wealth—the list is long.

But, encouraged by the apostles, the Christians learned to be what Christ had redeemed them to be, and the world changed. A new day had come. When people today say we need to get back to the good old days, they are thinking of the good old days after Christianity had spread far and wide, not the good old days that the first Christians found themselves living in. In those early days a new people, a redeemed people, reached out to a totally secular people and soon the Gospel had spread throughout the then-known world. The believers didn't join the world; the believers didn't fight against the world; the believers went into their world and proclaimed the Gospel just as Jesus had instructed them to do.

Will our current culture be reformed? Was the culture reformed after Isaac Backus called Christians to pray? Did the Second Great Awakening just happen or did God do a mighty work in answer to the earnest pleas of believers and their determination to be what Christ redeemed them to be? In short, reform of the culture begins with reform in the church.

When Revival Comes

When revival comes will the rough places be made smoother because we are doing the work that Isaiah talked about? And if Jesus should come back tomorrow, will He find us doing the kind of work He did when He walked the earth?

A study of history makes it difficult to claim that things in the world are worse today than in the past. Was the death of 50 million people during World War II insignificant? We have more people in our world, we have better news coverage of every atrocity that is committed, but are things worse now than ever before? The difference between the secular and the people of God has always been there and, at times, the evil in the world has been overwhelming. But isn't a lost and pagan culture exactly the culture where people can see a contrast between what is and what could be when Christ enters the hearts and lives of people?

What does the Lord of the church, the God of the ages, expect of us as we wait for our King's return? Is it to seek comfort for ourselves amidst all the chaos and decay surrounding us? Is it to engage in attempts to force darkness to behave as light so that our lives will be more comfortable? Or is it to be bringers of light to a dark world? Are we called to be pained lamenters or joyous announcers?

Henry Varley was a very good friend of D. L. Moody in the earlier days of Moody's evangelistic work. Moody loved to tell how Varley once said to him, "It remains for the world to see what the Lord can do with a man wholly consecrated to Christ." It is said that when Henry Varley spoke those words, Mr. Moody replied, "I will be that man." Moody told Varley, "Those were the words of the Lord through your lips to my soul." D. L. Moody believed the words of the Psalmist who told us that power belongs to God (see Ps. 62:11).

I am glad it does. I am glad that power did not belong to D. L. Moody; I am glad that it did not belong to Charles G. Finney; I am glad that it did not belong to Martin Luther; I am glad that it did not belong to any other Christian whom God has greatly used in this world's history. Power belongs to God. If D. L. Moody had any power, he got it from God.

Moody did not get that power by pushing for one political party over another or by calling for different laws. Moody did not get that power from quoting with authority the empty and often untrue words of media propagandists. Moody got his power from God. One man was used of God in mighty ways because he determined to be a man totally committed to Christ.

Revolutionize the Marketplace

One day I picked up the morning newspaper and saw another example of what seems to be an epidemic. It stated, "Two large hospital operators paid kickbacks to clinics that directed expectant mothers living in the U.S. illegally to their hospitals and filed fraudulent Medicaid claims on those patients." This was according to a whistleblower who called attention to the practice.

Would that have happened if the leaders caught making the fraudulent claims were Christians? We all know it could. Scandals in the past, whether in the great attempt at a silver monopoly or in companies like Enron, have involved business executives who declared that they were followers of Jesus. They claimed Christ but served mammon.

If Christians were behaving as the New Testament church behaved, with each looking out for others, each believer considering others ahead of himself and with Jesus at the center, would that make a difference in our culture? Would the marketplace be different if, through our obedience and faithfulness, God brought another Great Awakening?

Would the new marketplace still have a handful of people earning billions while workers sink further and further into poverty? Would subsidies offered by Congress go to the already rich business leaders while at the same time taking away food-stamp help from poor people—billions for the already rich, pennies for the working poor? Would that happen in a new day of God's Great Awakening?

Would the new marketplace put long-range research and development ahead of immediate executive bonuses so there would be a growing tomorrow for the marketplace? Would Christians stop supporting any who are usurious in order to help those who are the used? What will a new tomorrow look like?

Will those who shut down the government on October 1, 2013, be able to answer their constituents and God? When the government was shut down and the congressional leaders were told by the angry public that they shouldn't get paid until they worked together, one Republican congressman from Nebraska said that he wasn't going to give up his salary because, "I've got a nice house and a kid in college, and I'll tell you, we cannot handle it." Others explained why their congressional gym stayed open because, "We work hard and need it." Even so, there were complaints that not enough staff was working and there were no clean towels in the gym. What would Jesus say to them? Will this still be the way of thinking in another Great Awakening? Will selfishness, the me-centeredness of the nominal Christian, be the same in a new tomorrow?

Learning from Others

When I start to feel sorry for myself, or complain about there being economic difficulties that don't change for me just because I am a follower of Jesus, I think of others I have met who have so little. They are my teachers.

One day, when I was teaching at Daystar University in Nairobi, Kenya, one of my students asked if he could talk with me. We were breaking for lunch so I asked him to join me. This man was a pastor, a farmer and a student at the university. He came to class every day wearing a white shirt that was always spotless. His wife must have washed and ironed that shirt every night in preparation for the next day. It was also patched in many places. I bought my lunch and sat down with him at one of the tables. He had nothing in front of him. I asked, "Are you not eating?" He replied no, he would just visit. A few minutes later I asked again if he wanted lunch. No, he said. Then I finally figured it out and I asked, "Would you eat lunch with me if I pay for it?" Yes, he would, and I went to the line and purchased another plate. He ate ravenously. That plate of food cost me 37 cents. He didn't have it. But he wasn't complaining or lamenting that life was unfair or even that others seem to have enough to pay for a 37-cent meal. He was focused on his calling, his service to Christ, and was doing what he had to do to care for his family, his church and to be better educated so that he would have even more to offer the people he served. That day, as I saw his world through his circumstances, he was my teacher.

While I was teaching in Kiev, Ukraine, a Romanian pastor told me how things were in his family. He wasn't seeking my sympathy. In fact, he was praising the Lord for His goodness. He told me that he had twin grown daughters, both of them blind, living at home. He and his wife were caring for them. He told me, "As a pastor I earn $100 per month." Then wistfully he said, "If I were a doctor, I would be earning $400 per month." I could only listen. There was nothing I could say. He was doing so much to take the Gospel to his world and doing it with so little in return. He was my teacher.

I remember being in Calcutta, India, where the nighttime population was almost a million people greater than the daytime population. These were people who lived on the streets—sleeping, cooking and trying to keep clean with only the streets for their toilets. They were the ones going out into the fields and other places of work each morning, returning to their street place after dark. All day, 12–14 hours they toiled to earn enough to buy the rice they needed to feed their families their one meal of the day.

Yet when I listen to some of my American neighbors I hear things like, "Well, if those people weren't so lazy, they'd have what I have. I got mine the old fashioned way; I earned my wealth." But I have yet to see any of those who speak this way working the long hours, doing the backbreaking work, often in the hot sun, that those poor people endured. The point is, we live in a land of opportunity with available education and jobs where we don't have to work from sunup to sunset for enough money to buy one meal of rice. What would Jesus say about them and about us when we live in the same world? Do those people in their poverty matter to God? And, to make me pause and wonder, I've been learning recently that the Gospel is spreading in India in ways that are not occurring in my own prosperous land.

A level marketplace does provide opportunity for hard work. A level marketplace doesn't allow for businesses fleeing particular communities until those left behind live in blight, can't get out to the suburbs to find the jobs that moved there and can't even get out beyond the ghetto to buy food at the lower prices where many markets compete. So the poor get poorer with no way to escape. Then we label them "lazy" for their poverty and living conditions. We don't call them untouchables, as people who live on the streets of Calcutta are usually called, but we too often treat them that way. In our own spheres of influence are we creating a new Calcutta or a Christian community?

Which community would Jesus visit if He were to come among us? Which person would Jesus invite to eat with Him? Much is said in Scripture about the poor. Some Christians are becoming more aware of the divergence in wealth and opportunity and show concern and care. But not all do. Too many Christians still echo the culture that calls poor people lazy or, if they steal for bread, they are called "criminals." Which side of the great wealth divide do the followers of Jesus come down on? Which side would they come down on if there were another Great Awakening so that we looked at God and His teaching with new eyes and obeyed Him on His terms? Would such Christians still be asked by those who are observing us, "Why don't Christians follow their Founder"?

A Kingdom That Cannot Be Shaken

There is much to be learned from brothers and sisters in Christ who are being martyred in ever-increasing numbers in our world. Those who know them and look at their absolute faith tell us that in America one of our problems as Christians is that we are content to make do with a very little bit of God. For our brethren being martyred, commitment is the freedom that comes from no longer having anything but God.

Naghmeh Abedini, whose husband Saeed was sent to an Iranian prison because of his faith in Christ, explains that although in Western Christendom we want to isolate ourselves from hardship, pain, trial and difficulty, it is not so for the martyrs. They embrace their suffering; they do not run from it. They are a people who cannot be shaken. They have nothing left to lose. It was because of such people that the church grew so quickly in its early years. I have to ask myself if I will be ready if that day should come for me.

We are shaken by wars and natural disasters, we are shaken by broken health and financial reverses, we are shaken by destroyed relationships and broken government—but that isn't the end of our story. "We are receiving a kingdom that cannot be shaken" (Heb. 12:28). There could well be coming a new tomorrow as Christians refocus.

Even as believers have to live in the moment, our view of life is greater than that moment. We live in two kingdoms, the one that is on earth and dying and the one that isn't on earth and is living. The first will crumble; the second never will. For, like Abraham of old, we are "...looking forward to the city with foundations, whose architect and builder is God" (Heb. 11:10).

Didn't those who went before us also believe that they were in the last days? Didn't the apostle Paul sense that his were the days before the soon return of Christ? The point is not that we should stop anticipating, longing for the day. The point is that since we are that much closer to that day we should be working while there is still some time remaining. Those early believers who spoke of the coming again of Jesus, and expected it daily, were also the ones who gave their all each day for the Christ for whom they waited. Those who most anticipate the return of Christ tomorrow are the ones who serve the coming King with complete abandonment today.

Our job is neither to hide from the evil world nor to spend all our time lamenting how evil it is. Our calling is to, "Go into all the world and preach the gospel to all creation" (Mk. 16:15).

Our work is to redeem the time within the circumstances where God has placed us, just as faithful believers in the past have done.

Light a Candle

In a new tomorrow, will I spend all my time complaining about the darkness that is around me or will I light a candle? Will I walk an extra distance to escape the Samaritans in my world or will I go to them with the message of Jesus who also went through Samaria?

In the world where God has placed me I would rather work with the person who is totally opposed to God than the one who sort of agrees with me but is not really interested. Cold can become hot because there is already feeling and interest there. Lukewarm is very difficult to work with. I live in trust that the Holy Spirit will bring along those persons who are spiritually ready for His Good News. Most people already know that they cannot fix themselves. Certainly by the time most people reach maturity they already know where most of the dead ends are in their world; they've already found them. Our little candles may be all the light they need to start their journey toward wholeness and peace in Christ. I am going to light a candle today, I am going to light a candle tomorrow, and I will keep on lighting candles and keep placing them on a lampstand. And if, in the past, there has been a bushel basket over my candle, I will make sure that tomorrow that bushel basket will no longer be there. The light needs to shine.

For me, right now, where I am, in my situation, I will exclaim with the Psalmist, "This is the day that the LORD has made; let us rejoice and be glad in it" (Ps. 118:24, ESV). I will seek to live as God wants me to live, "Not by might, nor by power, but by my Spirit, says the LORD Almighty" (Zech. 4:6). I will not add to this the words, "by my politics, by my petitions or by my anger."

Ready for a New Awakening

Are we examples of the kind of people we want in our nation? If the culture revels in decadence, do Christians revel in it too? There is enough evidence to show that many of us do and are seen by the secular people who watch us as a hypocritical people. Are we praying, seeking the God who changes everything while He Himself never changes? Or have we acclimated and become part of the world system that we claim we so much despise? Is there any difference between us and the culture we rail against? Before looking at "them," which too often keeps us from looking at ourselves, we need to look at our own behavior and the attitudes that drive our behavior.

Is it pornography? To those who have nothing better in their lives, nothing more, the degradation of pornography is an escape. But why would Christians who have the "so much more" that others lack trade it for so much less? Yet too many do. The stories about pastors watching porn on out-of-town trips still draws the attention of those who ache for men of God to be faithful.

Is it free and open sex? Surveys show that 75 percent of the culture sees living together without marriage as a normal behavior. That follows along with neither knowing what marriage is as God designed it nor what marriage can be under the guidance of the God of love. The culture doesn't know what God offers but many professing believers don't know either and can neither tell about it nor demonstrate it. Statistics don't show a great difference between the behavior of those who claim to be redeemed and those who are among the lost.

And what can we say about the worship of money, prestige, the worship of things that can never satisfy? We are saying loud and clear to the culture around us, "You are wrong in what you do but we don't have anything better to offer because in one way or another we are following after you and doing the same things that you are doing."

In her book *The New Faithful*, Colleen Carroll says, "Studies of fundamentalist and evangelical churches have found that their members divorce at the same or higher rates than the general population. And in many parts of the Protestant Bible Belt, the divorce rate is roughly 50 percent higher than the national average. A study by the Princeton University Center for Research on Child Wellbeing found that Southern Baptist couples are more likely to divorce than the general population."

Biblical orthodoxy starts with those who claim it and want it. Maybe Colleen Carroll has found something when she states, "…interviews of the young believers…seem to indicate that this generation craves mystery and connection to the traditions that the modern world has stripped away."

This may be indicative of the need for what today's young people feel in that they have had churches appeal to them in every way that copies the ways and means of the surrounding culture whereas they are looking for the mystery, the otherness of God, the Holy One who reaches down to us but is not one of us. The holiness of God has been ignored for so long, the judgment of God pushed aside, that the idea of what was once thought of as old is new again. What is biblical is being looked at with new eyes. Maybe, in a Christian culture that has made God into a good buddy who sees things our way, what people are seeking now is what people have always sought—the God who is other.

When God Breaks Out

We serve a God who surprises. Just when we think we have God in a box, to do what we want Him to do according to our wishes and to do it our way, whether it is getting our favorite political candidate elected or stopping some human-hurting cultural trend, God will do what God sees best to do. He is God; we are not and never will be.

Faithful believers seek not to manipulate God but pray to be in the pathway of His movements. Who wants us to follow Him more than He does? Who aches for the social enslavements that cripple people who engage in all the perversions that mankind seems so able to invent? Who still calls, "Come to me, all you who are weary and burdened, and I will give you rest. Take my yoke upon you and learn from me, for I am gentle and humble in heart, and you will find rest for your souls. For my yoke is easy and my burden is light" (Matt. 11:28–30)?

That's the Christ that so many in our culture aren't seeing. That's the Christ whom too many of us have buried under so much that isn't of Him. That's the Christ the culture needs. And that's the Christ we need when we say we are following Him now but so often have been following everything else instead of Him.

The more we see how God has surprised men and women in the past by doing "…immeasurably more than all we ask or imagine, according to his power that is at work within us…" (Eph. 3:20) the more likely we are to surrender our own agendas and begin watching for His.

Some evangelical Christians, including those who consider themselves evangelical leaders, have forgotten who God is. They want Omnipotence to give way to their own ability to make things happen; they prefer that Omnipresence give way to their belief that they can do wonders though their own organizations or communication systems to make the culture become what they want it to be. They want Omniscience to give way to what their own ideas determine is important and what is not.

If we stop promoting ourselves and our own agendas, and seek once more to be people of the Way, will there once again be a Great Awakening? When I stop thinking that everything centers around me and what I do and, by implication, that there is little God can do, especially if I am no longer on the scene for God to use; or if I can think only about end times and my own great escape, I may not care about God's renewal, His bringing change to people and the world. If I think that without me God can do nothing and all possibilities end with my death, that the end of my life is the end of history, I won't care much about the great movement of God that may yet be ahead. But if I hurt for others and long for the touch of God on our world, even if I don't live to see it, then maybe I will at last abandon myself and pray for the will of the One who will never abandon us.

The end may be near; God knows. Or tomorrow may be a whole new morning. A new Great Awakening will depend on our being open to the power and resources of God. It means being watchful and awake to all that is happening in our culture, our neighbors, and our political situations. And it means being surrendered to God's direction in our lives so that each of us can say with the prophet, "Here am I, send me" (see Isaiah 6:8).

A People Divided

Jesus has always divided people. That shouldn't come as a surprise. The apostle John tells us that "…the people were divided because of Jesus" (see John 7:43). That is just as true now as it was then. There are secular people, there are religious people and there are followers of Jesus. There is no overlap in God's eyes. Some of the most secular people may be closer to the kingdom than they think. And some of the most "religious" may be further away. It is often much easier to talk about the Savior to someone who is totally opposed to the Christian faith than it is to talk to one who has made the Savior what he wants Him to be on his own terms. Love and hate are often extremes of the same emotion. It is often the lukewarm person or the semi-Christian who is the hardest to reach.

God doesn't give up on people, and I can't either. But I may, in my zeal to bring in more about Christ than He taught about Himself, keep from Him the very people who deep down inside recognize that they are missing out, feeling empty, wanting more in this life that doesn't satisfy or fulfill. I don't want to be the kind of professing Christian who keeps others away from the Savior.

We have drifted, so many of us. We have left what is most important for something less. In all my conversations with unbelievers, I hear far more negatives about the apparent disconnect between what the Bible teaches and how evangelical Christians think and act than I do about the Gospel message itself. It is so easy to get in the way, to clutter our Gospel with what is neither biblical nor true. I read the words of the prophet Isaiah, "The people walking in darkness have seen a great light; on those living in the land of deep darkness a light has dawned" (Isaiah 9:2). Then I ask myself, "Will the people around me see that great light?"

Look At Those Who Went before Us

Where was the early church placed when it grew so fast and the Gospel message spread so far? They were living in a pagan culture where to acknowledge Christ, and not Zeus or Apollo or Diana, was to lose all the rights of citizenship. The way the Christians lived was as counter-culture persons within the existing culture. They didn't try to copy the culture's political, social or legal ways in order to try to change the culture. They knew where real change came from. They knew who gave them a new heart and a new way of thinking and behaving. The early believers were examples of the love of God in human flesh. They lived the life without assuming that they should try to force the pagan culture to accommodate them. They knew who they were. They did not try to serve two masters.

It is time for us to refocus. If we want to be in harmony with God's Holy Spirit and be men and women who are faithful, our thinking has to be turned back to God. In the last book of the Bible, the apostle John spoke of the Pergamum church. Those early Christians were told, "I know where you live—where Satan has his throne" (Rev. 2:13).

Where were those first-century Christians living? They were living right where Satan seemed to be king and where so many in that culture were bowing down to him. Are we also living in a world where Satan seems to have his throne? Are the people around us bowing down to Satan? Why are we surprised by that? Why do we think life should be different for us than it was for those early believers who went before us? Why do we assume that those who bow down to Satan should stop doing that so we won't be offended and life around us will be the way we want it to be?

Pergamum was known as a place given over to idolatry. Behind the city there was a hill that was covered with heathen temples. The chief one was the temple of Zeus. So God called that place "Satan's seat." It was the place of Satan's throne.

Think about that. We can look at our circumstances, our world, the pressures, the struggles, the things over which we have no control but that are influencing our lives. The Lord tells us, "I know where you live." Where did we ever get the idea that God doesn't know where we live and that we have to take matters into our own hands and become known as an angry, militant people who seem to think that if anything is going to change we have to change it? And why will we follow aspects of the culture that uses lies in order to accomplish its own ends? What if the people of Pergamum had done in their day what too many Christians are doing in our day? What would our Lord have said about that?

Sometime, try making a list of all the things that are having an impact on your life. God knows about every item on that list; you are not living here on your own. It isn't just that He is saying, "I know you." He is saying, "I know where you live."

There were negatives about that Pergamum church. God knew it and through John reminded them of where they had compromised. Some of those Christians were placing a stumbling block in front of others. It wasn't a new stumbling block either; it had been a stumbling block among some of the people of ancient Israel. In spite of our good intentions, when we add to the Gospel our own social and political teachings, we too are capable of placing a stumbling block in front of others.

But there was a positive for the Pergamum church too. Here it is: "Yet you remain true to my name." In that place where Satan had his throne, the believers remained true to His name. Will that be said of us as we live in a culture that is not Christian—even a place where Satan seems to have his throne? Will we be known by others as a people true to His name? Or, will we be known as something else, something other than the people who are true to His name?

I can rail against all that is wrong, try to use secular means to overcome what I see is unbiblical, or I can stay faithful to Jesus. The early church had to make that decision; so do we.

Stay or Go?

Am I ready to go with God tomorrow if that is the last day and God writes, "Finished"? Or am I ready to stay with God here if the last day is not yet? Am I ready to enter my world and its culture in the power of God or am I more interested in simply lamenting how bad things are around me and point to who I think might be responsible? Have I forgotten what God's Word tells us, "'We know that the whole creation has been groaning as in the pains of childbirth right up to the present time" (Rom. 8:22)?

Have I somehow drifted to the conclusion that if people try hard enough, or vote the correct way, they can behave as redeemed Christians without being redeemed by Jesus? Do I really think that we who are a part of this fallen world can correct what is wrong by the ballot box or with our guns? Have I forgotten that only God can make all things new?

If I am to stay here in this world, what then of my tomorrows? Will I go into tomorrow crying about what is, as if God is blind to what I see around me? Or will I acknowledge the power of God, as D. L. Moody did, and place myself in God's hands to be used by Him as a light-bearer for the sake of those who live in darkness?

Scripture's imperatives drive me. Just because "The fool says in his heart, 'There is no God'" (Psalm 14:1), doesn't make the words of that fool correct. Nor is that a reason to reject that person who says, "There is no God." Rather, that is a call to be concerned for the soul of that person. We can't help but long for that person any more than we can help wanting a person with cancer to be cured or a destitute person to find food and shelter. It matters to us.

The apostle Paul asked, "Has not God made foolish the wisdom of the world?" (1 Cor. 1:20). Of course He has. That is why this moment counts if this is the very moment that God has arranged when we meet the person who has only his secular mind to guide him. He may think that his foolish mind is sufficient to make it in this life. We know that his personal sufficiency will never bring him to where he needs to be or fulfill the emptiness that tells him something is missing in his life. We long for him to find his rightful place in a world made by God, functioning by the rules given by God. The incomplete person has no idea that he is incomplete. He just knows, in his honest moments, that something isn't right. I can speak to that because

I remember confessing to that same sense of lack years before I came to meet the living Christ.

I have to look at myself. As a Christian, if I only worship "my faith," "my doctrines," my ideas about what is true for me, my politics and my concepts of a right society, and my views about who is and who is not acceptable to God, I may miss that great tomorrow of God. God will act, but I will be on the sidelines missing out on what the Spirit of God is doing. But if I am open to the work of the living, reigning God in Christ, tomorrow I may enter into God's next Great Awakening. What that will be like I cannot even imagine.

One of the greatest movements of God ever to happen in our world may just be starting. The Christian who is focused on God will be ready for it. The Christian who instead is focused on everything else may be sidelined. Each believer has a choice to make—God or politics, Jesus or the culture. We cannot worship both.

Come Quickly

Most of us have heard the lament, "We are at the end of the Christian Era." Or, as some put it, "The Lord has to be coming soon because things here are so bad."

Who is Lord of the church and who decides when the Lord will return? It isn't me or any of my fellow believers. We can look for His coming, and we should. We can regret the state of the culture, and that regret is legitimate. But it may be that God has a new plan, as so often He has had in the past.

To the One who says, "Yes, I am coming soon," we reply, "Come, Lord Jesus" (Rev. 22:20). I look for that soon-coming of Christ. Certainly the world has not improved since that cry was first made. Life is easier but not necessarily better. Yet so many other believers down through history have prayed that same prayer. We think, "Surely all that is happening around us is indicative of the last days or end times." It is true, we are in the last days; we are in the end times. We have been since Jesus ascended into heaven, leaving behind His promise to return and sending the Holy Spirit to guide us. We think too many years have gone by, but that is by our time-measuring standard. God has a different standard.

The returning Christ may put everything in motion before the next minute passes. We live in anticipation of that. So have all believers at all times, many who lived through and were even martyred in times far worse than our own. We think no one has ever faced what we face, but they have. As believers have done for two thousand years we look for Christ's coming, we work now while we can, we are faithful to the One to whom we will give an account, and we don't surrender to the ways of a culture that is going to be in a tough place when that last day is here. The former prostitute, Rehab, had a scarlet cord to mark her place. We have the protecting Holy Spirit and the mark of the One who calls us His own. Rehab didn't go out and engage in political protests. She did what she promised to do and she and her household were spared. Have I put out my scarlet cord?

Until that day when Christ returns we may be on the verge of a third Great Awakening. We don't want to miss it. God is a God of mercy, love and surprises. His next revival may be just a day or two away from starting. If that new day is similar to other awakenings that came in the midst of earlier decadent cultures that surrounded the believers, what a great day that is going to be.

With the Time I Have Left

The apostle Paul challenges and encourages us with the prayer "...that the God of our Lord Jesus Christ, the glorious Father, may give you the Spirit of wisdom and revelation, so that you may know him better. I pray that the eyes of your heart may be enlightened in order that you may know the hope to which he has called you, the riches of his glorious inheritance in his holy people" (Eph. 1:17–18).

With whatever time God gives me on earth before He says, "It's time to leave now; come on Home," I want to be focused on what matters. I am a citizen of my country but I am also a citizen of heaven. If I am going to be a faithful citizen, I have to be a person of truth in all that I do and in all that I say. I have to be true to His name.

With that clear determination of knowing who we are and to whom we belong, we move out into our culture with the caring love of Jesus. And if our focus has been lost, it is time to return to God and to what He teaches. It is time once again to be known in our culture by what God has called us to be—"Christ Ones."

Made in the USA
Lexington, KY
24 February 2014